M000191977

KNOWING

SANDRINE BAPTISTE
AND RHONDA
TREMAINE

KNOWING

The Secret Power
of Flow
Manifesting

© 2021 ENoetic Press

Copyright © 2021 by Sandrine Baptiste and Rhonda
Tremaine   Cover Design: Ian Tremaine

All rights reserved. No portion of this book may be used or
reproduced in any form, or by any means, without written
permission from the authors except as permitted by the fair
use rule. For permissions, or to order bulk copies of this material, write to enp@everythingnoetic.com

This book is intended to inform, educate and provide support for spiritual development solely based on the research,
opinions and experiences of the authors. It is not meant to
provide counselling or medical advice, and the information
contained in this book should not be construed or used as a
substitute for advice from a licensed professional including
but not limited to a physician, a counselor, a psychologist,
or a psychiatrist.

The mention of specific theories, individuals, organizations,
or products is for reference only or for the purpose of example and should not be construed as an endorsement of a
concept, an author, an organization, or a product. The
reader assumes all risks for actions taken in association
with ideas from such mentions. The authors and publisher
assume no responsibility or liability to any person or entity
with respect to any loss, damages or injury caused or alleged
to be caused directly or indirectly by any information contained in this book. Examples used in this book are fictious.
Any example that appears to be based on a person, living or
dead, is purely coincidental. The authors and publisher have
made every effort, at the time of publication, to ensure that
this book's information is correct and they assume no responsibility for any actions that result, directly or indirectly,
from errors or omissions. The authors make no claims nor
do they provide guarantees, warranties, or assurances of any
kind, whether expressed or implied.

First printing, March 2022.
Library of Congress Control Number: 2021907885
ISBN: 978-0-9858647-3-6   eISBN: 978-0-9858647-4-3

Dedication

We dedicate this book to our first families, especially our mothers and fathers, who raised us, and made this physical journey possible.

We also dedicate this book to the children—especially Noah, Ava and John—who understand the simplicity of the moment, continually exhibit curiosity and joy and who are closest to the truth of who we really are.

But mostly, we dedicate this book to you, dear reader, because our mission is to promote the benefits of self-knowledge and to encourage well-being for the purpose of creating a better world. We hope you find the material enlightening and begin to discover the peace within, something that comes with the understanding

of who we really are and that we are all connected.

CONTENTS

CONTENTS

Preface

Dear Reader,

I was manifesting before it was popular and before it was called that. I was a Nichiren Shoshu Buddhist during the 1970s. I practiced diligently for four years, chanting several times a day for whatever I wanted. During the early days of this sect of Buddhism that made its way to the USA, the rules were pretty loose. We were taught to chant for whatever we desired and you know what? I did get everything I wanted, pretty much. I manifested a relationship that lasted, money that didn't, and a career that went through a number of changes, and then I stopped chanting and was sort of like a regular person. I got married and had a family. I got baptized and went to church, attended bible study groups and prayed.

Sometimes my prayers were answered, but I did go through ups and downs and held on to little else but faith. And then around the year 2000, I leveraged the typical New Age practices to manifest. Through these experiences, I learned that we can put it out there and get something back, but more often than not, what we think we want really isn't. In other words, life is fluid and our desires do a one-eighty, like all the time. And I learned that you cannot manifest the important things by wishing them into existence. I actually learned this experientially through practicing Buddhism. The reason why I got what I wanted almost all of the time was that I was in alignment with the universe. My life condition was strong. It all started with me, and not with anything out in the world, and not with any kind of magic.

Today, Sandrine and I teach what we refer to as Flow Manifesting. That is, we teach you how to strengthen your core, work with your higher self and basically, go with the flow of life. You are part of the flow and when you are aligned, you are able to attract all the good into your life. If you already believe in the Law of Attraction, you know that like attracts like. Good energy. Good stuff.

So relax. Read this book slowly. Do the exercises and you will get there. There really is no secret to Flow Manifesting, but it is a process. Change your thoughts and beliefs. Work with your emotions. Meditate. Get over every one of your fears, even the fear of death and it is so simple you will not even believe it! So maybe it is kind of a secret, but it's more of a mind shift. Once you know the truth, you will be able to relax into your current life and incrementally make changes for the better. And best of all, you will feel good about your life, no matter what is going on around you.

Rhonda

Dear Reader,

When you are a child, your world is small. You accept the outside world for what you perceive and do not question anything. You think that your experience is the same as everyone else's and it becomes your normalcy. You live in the present moment and do not anticipate the future, and your memories serve as landmarks for your life. You feel good in your routine, satisfying a few needs. Life is simple, life is enough, you can sense this *joie de vivre*, always there. It is a magical sensation that overcomes everything and brings you back to homeostasis. Life is good!

At least that's how I remember my childhood, except that my normalcy included memories of the future, which I never really questioned until I was a teenager, when I realized that not everyone had these.

Later, these memories appeared when I met people for the first time. How was I able to recognize someone I just met? How could I know the big lines for my life? Now I realize that I was in the flow or in alignment with my soul and able to sense and go in the direction of the universe. It all made sense. I was always an introvert so navigating my inner world was something I knew. I just needed to realize that not everyone is connected in that way.

Flow Manifesting is more than the Law of Attraction for those familiar with this concept. It is a spiritual awakening which requires a will to grow at the soul level and to understand what is happening inside of you. This awakening often begins when you feel a discrepancy between your inner world and outside reality. It is your first clue that you have to investigate.

In this book, we take you on a journey to discover your inner world, which is so necessary to the expansion and liberation of your soul. This walk through an understanding of who you are as an energy consciousness will help you to unlock the power within your subconscious mind that has kept you away from your path of enlightenment. This manuscript is the foundation of all of our teachings and a complete guide to living your full potential.

Ready, Set...Go!

Sandrine

CHAPTER

1

THE SOUL

When asked to tell someone who you are, do you start with your name and where you live and what you do for a living? It is common to do so. After all, that is how we identify ourselves. You may also elaborate on your job or expand on your personal ties and accomplishments, such as where you are from, who your family is, and what you like to do in your spare time. What we tell people is a reflection of how we see ourselves and the attributes we want to display. It is simpler to say something like *I am Bridget from Tuscaloosa and I love to watch movies* than to say you are a soul born in the current time-space reality just getting their shit together for the next go round. We said a mouthful. Yes, we implied that everyone has a soul and that we just happened to be born in this place and time, which suggests that there were other dimensions or time periods in which we might have been born at that exact moment, and yes, we did imply that reincarnation is a thing. But stay with us. We are not going to deliver an iron-clad philosophy or tell you to believe what we believe; we are going to ask you to find the answers to life's burning questions within yourself. Just like Dorothy in the *Wizard of Oz* had the answers inside of her all along--so do you!

Your soul, or the energy particles within you, is timeless and infinite. It has always been with you. And as science supports, it will never die because energy can neither be created nor destroyed. Deep inside, you know exactly what we are talking about. Perhaps you've heard it called the higher self or energy consciousness. The soul has been referred to in many ways. But it doesn't matter how you label it. Just understand that the energy is intangible and indefinable. It just is. And while the experience of the soul may be difficult to describe, you feel it. Some have an intimate knowledge of the soul because they deliberately get in touch with that part of themselves frequently through meditation.

Meditation is the human gateway to the soul as the practice helps you to experience a time when this energy was all you could sense. Before you were born, you were just this energy, and after you die you will once again be this energy, sometimes referred to as source or God. We refer to a piece of the larger energy field as a soul. It is not a specific, individual entity like the ego, but it is a unique expression of source energy. While each of our souls is a part of this larger energy consciousness, its essence is fused with the human part of us, the part of us that sees ourselves as individuals. So yes, we are one, but each soul has a distinct essence. You are you, but you are also source.

Many of us think of the soul as residing inside of our bodies. It is not really there physically, but it is the only way our human minds can comprehend this indescribable but utterly important presence. Therefore, we sometimes refer to going within or the inner self when describing the connection.

You may have experienced the presence of the soul while grieving for a loved one. Perhaps during such a time you remember the rest of the world dissolving, where you could only sense your breath and feel this energy. Life stopped for a moment and you were vulnerable but at the same time, stronger for it. For that moment, you were all that existed. The rest of the world had fallen away. Maybe you experienced a similar phenomenon during a serious illness or when you attempted a physical challenge. Each example is different, but in some ways they are all the same. In each example, you accessed this part of you in order to reduce your pain or reach the finish line. You were not pushing through--that's the ego. Rather, you were in touch with your soul because you knew, at that moment, there was nothing outside of yourself on which you could rely. At that moment, it was all about you, but it was not about your ego. It was about the connection to and expansion of your soul. And while such moments are infused with awe and revelation, the experience is rather subtle.

The soul is the part that whispers. It breaks through often unexpectedly in situations where you feel conflicted. The soul is that quiet voice you will easily miss if you do not pay attention. When you are connected, you feel a familiarity. You know this part of you. You have been here before. This place inside of you will never change--not ever-- and when you get in touch, you know this, but the soul is often not experienced through the five senses. Rather, it persists in spite of your humanness. It is not a feeling. It is a presence. Some see it as a quiet, personal sacred space. Meditation helps you to access this space. When you get in touch more often, and perhaps meditate as a daily practice, your world will change. We are not making an empty promise. Things will change through accessing this inner consciousness because everything that happens in this lifetime is intimately tied to the soul, and this is what we call knowing. This indescribable soul experience defies words. You have to live it! It cannot be learned from books or taking a class because when you experience something, it is real. Everything else is a product of the mind. Through this book, we try to explain it the best we can, but the knowing is the experience that, by definition, can only be evidenced through going within.

Once you are connected to the soul, you are more intuitive and are able to make better decisions for your life. You've probably heard spiritual thought teacher Marianne Williamson say something to the effect that you think you have a number of problems but you really only have one. Here, she suggests that your only problem is that you are not connected to God. And it makes sense to say that if you have a number of problems, you can resolve each one of them by going within and connecting with the energy. And so your only problem really is that you are shut off from this energy. When you are truly in touch with your soul, you will be able to uncover answers to what you think of as your problems because you will become more intuitive. Using your intuition, or your inner guidance system, will give you the solutions you seek every time. So if you have a question about your life's direction, or even if you can't decide on what to do right this minute, you can go within and follow your inner guidance. The more you get in touch with your soul, the more secure you will feel in the groundlessness that is the human experience and the better access you will have to the knowledge you seek to make the best decisions for your life.

When you are connecting frequently, you may also occasionally experience a spontaneous, blissful feeling of peace and love that overtakes your entire being for seemingly no reason. This is because the more you forge the connection, the more you are in touch with source energy, which is always blissful. This is a bonus of meditation. And while you will still have a range of emotions, some of them uncomfortable, you will be better equipped to handle the less joyful circumstances. With a meditation practice, you will be more centered and less reactionary. So when something negative comes into your life, you won't dwell on it because your vibration will be higher. In other words, when you start from a peaceful place, the downward spiral is less likely to happen. Meditation, along with the other practices in this book, will help you achieve the peace of mind you seek.

Not only will connecting with the higher energy provide relief from negative feelings, you will become more creative. The soul is where the juice of creativity resides and where you feel alive and passionate about what you are doing. It is that undeniable knowing coming from source that guides you forward when you are writing, painting, dancing or creating in other ways. *Eat Pray Love* author Elizabeth

Gilbert's 2009 TED Talk focused on the elusive creative genius that lives inside each one of us. In the talk, Gilbert suggests that creativity is something on loan to you from an unimaginable source. Indeed, it is not our human thinking selves initiating these ideas, though our egos would like to think so, but rather, the inspiration come from a higher energy.

And it is certainly logical to conclude that if we are all connected to a single energy field, the ideas may spring from there, rather than our human minds. And if you are a creative, you already know this. You need inspiration in order to work, and when that inspiration comes, it's a bolt of lightning. Then, using your mind that perceives things in a unique way, you create the finished product and send it out into the world. The end result is your personal, creative expression but its origin is the source energy that moves through you. So when you paint or write or compose, you do not sit down and think. You sit down and wait for the ideas to flow and that comes from the connection to your soul.

The soul also prompts you to recognize the oneness in the world, facilitating a connectedness to everyone, and to nudge a realization that love is the most important thing there is. Love is the recognition of source energy in yourself or another person. It infuses you with the desire to give more and to be nice to the people around you. The soul creates magic, facilitating the instant and intrinsic understanding that we are part of one another. When you understand this, your needs, wants and expectations change because it is not just about you anymore.

Once you realize you are part of the collective, your world expands and you become more accepting of other human beings, who each have their own unique perception. Knowing who you are--a spirit being in a human body--helps to put things into perspective. Without this knowledge, we would allow our wandering thoughts, pure emotion and controlling egos to wreak havoc in our lives. This is because as human beings, we live our lives largely through the mind.

Many of us have an idea of what the mind is, but it is hard to nail down a precise dictionary definition of "mind" as it is an abstract concept. When we use the term, we are talking about multiple possibilities. The thinking, rational mind, the part of the mind that is able to solve problems and design buildings and cook an incredibly difficult dish with precision, is the aware mind. That is, when you are concentrating your efforts on one thing, and not thinking about anything else, you are aware. You are at your best, and the reason is because you are conscious.

When we use the term conscious or consciousness we are not referring to a state of mind opposite a physically unconscious state. Rather, we are talking about a state of mind that is opposite the automated mind, or the mind that continually thinks the same thoughts over and over again. In some ways, when you are in this state of "automated," where your mind goes off on tangents and creates disharmony, you are using your mind, but you are sort of unconscious. That is, there is no awareness of what you are doing, no thought as to how to solve a problem, no ability to really listen to another human being. Rather, your mind is all over the place, thinking random thoughts and not really present. When this happens—and it is how most people are most of the time—you are not only not accomplishing anything, you are often creating unnecessary drama for yourself. So, for us, the aware mind exists in the present and when thinking happens, it is willfully directed. Yet, perhaps the most important reason why the aware mind acts so intelligently is because you are connected to the soul. You are outside of your babbling mind and rather, forging a connection with the deeper part of yourself. So when you are thinking in this state of mind, you are drawing on the soul's knowledge. You are drawing conclusions with the rational mind fused with your intuition and it is this state of awareness that creates wise decision-making and contentment.

Another important concept is the ego—the part of the mind that distinguishes us from other human beings and continually fights to be center stage. It is the part of us that establishes our personal identity and attaches itself to many of our thoughts, which prompts us to identify with them. Such an identification impedes us from developing a stronger relationship with the soul. So in order to deepen the relationship with the soul, you need to let go of the ego long enough to allow the meaningful connection to take place. That is, you should attempt to detach from it whenever it is spewing repetitive and useless information. You will know this is happening when you are not in imminent danger, but you are thinking negative thoughts. Sometimes, it is obvious because the thoughts are relentless. Your mind repeats negative information over and over again as if you were not listening the first time and these thoughts can only be properly dealt with through getting into a state of awareness.

This is a process that will need to be done repeatedly. It is not a one and done. You will shift from thinking negatively to awareness and back again, but once the connection with your soul develops and grows, you will be centered more frequently. You will feel better more often and all the good things you want will flow into your life one way or another in a manner and in a time frame that is aligned with your highest good.

Once you are able to turn the volume down on your unconscious thoughts, you will begin to notice synchronicities, the feeling of joy more often, and an inner knowing that helps you to make the right decisions. You begin to connect with your intuition at will. Sometimes, we need to think about things mindfully in a state of awareness to reach a conclusion, but other times, the knowing comes as a gut feeling. How intuition manifests has a lot to do with your unique connection with the soul. And while you will certainly forge this connection if you look for it, and you may even feel on top of the world at times, what you need to also understand is that the high will not last. Sometimes, you will be in perfect alignment and feel really good, but you also need to accept the fragility of the human condition. You can never lose the connection, but you will have to deal with your ego constantly. Once you know who you are as a soul, and a human, your capacity to live fully will be enhanced and only then, will you be able to create the satisfying life you seek.

ON BEING HUMAN

What does it mean to be human? According to science, human beings, or Homo sapiens, evolved from now extinct predecessors, or if you want to believe the Bible we were created by God, or if you want to believe a combination of the two, there are explanations as to how both can be correct, but again, belief is just, well, a belief. And the precise definition of human being, or its evolution, is not important anyway. We just want to be clear that, for us, being human means having a physical body but it is also associated with consciousness or the soul.

Of course, that physical body involves a human brain, one that is different from other animals. Birds, bees, lions and tigers largely live by instinct rather than their minds. They don't worry. They live in the moment. But as humans, we use our minds at a higher level. We tend to make decisions based on thought and we are able to self-reflect and analyze our choices. This is a decided advantage as humans have the capacity to build permanent structures, create social institutions, and develop scientific innovations and our lives are easier for it. We have clothing and homes and all sorts of material goods. We have created so many things with our human minds, but as we already stated, there are detrimental effects when they dominate. To get a better grasp of this concept, let's take a look at how we as human beings are born into this corporeal existence, which starts with the first breath of life.

The moment of birth

The moment of birth is a milestone, marking your presence on the earth plane in a particular time and place and in a particular body. Your soul, your physical body and the DNA that programs it, fuses with your experiences--even in the first months of life-- making you uniquely you. An astrology chart--also known as the natal chart--marks the occasion. Some astrologers refer to the chart as the karmic blueprint of the soul but it also provides information about your personality, physical appearance and how you interact with the world. And while astrology can help you to distinguish yourself from others, in some way, all human beings are alike. They are the same in how their bodies look, function and behave, but just as there are species-specific commonalities, there are also vast differences largely determined by DNA. You can easily see this by looking around. You'll see people of all different heights and weights as well as pigment variations in their skin, hair and eyes. DNA is the material that carries the genetic code creating such characteristics; it gives us the tendency to develop certain diseases and is also a behavioral influencer. Of course, there are exceptions like identical twins, where physical characteristics are so similar, people have trouble distinguishing one from the other. Still, close friends and relatives usually do not have much trouble telling those that look similar apart as there are unique characteristics such as voice, speech patterns, weight differences and things acquired along the way like tattoos, glasses, clothing preferences and hair style. Also, while identical twins carry the same genetic material, each possess subtle unique physical features, and personality will be affected by environment, even when raised together. Regardless of physical appearance, every single person has a unique essence, and that is where the soul comes in.

The imprint of the soul is stronger than both physical DNA and environment. You know that, right? When you are connected to the soul, you discover your passions. You know just what you want to do and how you want to do it. You listen to that small but powerful inner voice and when you are truly connected, it gives you the strength to act in unexpected ways. For example, perhaps you come from a long line of carpenters and builders and in fact, everyone works well with their hands in your family tree. There is a sense of pride in the trade. But you come along and you want to be a dancer. This likely angers your parents who wanted you to take over the family business. So why did you break the mold? The answer is simple. You listened to your soul.

Life and how it works

Think of yourself as an entity that is part human and part soul. The soul has free will and it understands that we have choices. Part of choosing is listening to the wisdom of the ego while not letting it shut out the inner sense of who we really are. Again, the ego is the part of the mind that is responsible for personal identity. It distinguishes us from others so that we can live on the planet as distinct human beings.

The ego is very necessary because we are individuals and need to have names and other personally identifiable information to live in the world. The ego, along with the rest of the mind, helps us to figure out how we should behave in society. Amongst other things, it helps us avoid imprisonment and accidental death because those random, negative thoughts going through your head are often about dangers and some of those warnings should be heeded. The mind sifts through information from conscious thoughts to what dwells in the unconscious. It comes to conclusions and if the mind is working while in a state of awareness, the conclusions are likely the best for you. It does not mean that you ever have the truth as in this physical world we co-create, much has to do with perception and even if there is an objective reality in the physical world, it is often a reality we will never know cerebrally. We can only interpret information in our minds and therefore, our conclusions are always subjective. It is not as if the soul has the answers to our physical world problems either. It is a non-physical, non-human energy. However, because it is a pure, positive life-force, the conclusions you reach will be better for you.

That the soul connection is always better than solely listening to your mind does not mean that you will avoid error in your conclusions. You may be in a state of awareness, but you are also influenced by outside forces, your wandering mind, and past programming. The more you are connected, the more objective you will be and the more you will draw on intuition than succumb to your fears or old patterns. You may know what your soul is telling you already because you are aware of your true passions and desires, but again, listening to your soul does not mean shutting out the ego. Maybe your soul is here to create music or play tennis, but if you find you cannot make a living at it, you need a day job. So we will not suggest that you quit your job to pursue your dream. That's insane. Nor will we tell you to wish your life into being without actually doing anything. Life doesn't work that way because while we are powerful beings with extraordinary mystical capabilities, we are living in a physical world with an economic framework. That is the duality. Additionally, we share the planet with many many other human beings who co-create with us. Because of our differences, and the fact that our ability to earn money is often tied to other people, our intentions will not necessarily materialize in the way that we think. So if you have bills to pay, you need to consider how you are going to earn a living while pursuing your passion.

To get to where you want to be, you need to be practical while holding tight to the dream. Some of the early years may be filled with a lot of juggling, hard work and grit, but think of it this way: if you set an intention, and move toward your goal, you will be doing what needs to be done to achieve the rock star status you desire, while also taking care of your responsibilities. It's a win-win.

And here's another thing to consider. You are doing your day job for a reason, even if you do not understand the reason yet. When you work your day job, you meet people and have experiences that likely contribute to the lessons you are here to learn. Relationships at work, though they seem trivial in nature compared to friendships and familial ties, are often vital for our personal development. Work situations bring up issues of morality, test our resilience, challenge us in ways our close personal relationships do not, and provide avenues of growth, even if that job is not something we associate with a calling.

So if you knew you were doing what you were supposed to be doing--and you are--you can give up thinking, if only I had gone to law school, if only I pursued an engineering degree, if only I had taken that job in New York or Tokyo or Paris or wherever. The point is that you are here doing what you are supposed to be doing in this lifetime where you can use your present experiences for growth. And you can, and should, pursue anything and everything else you want to do too, simultaneously.

But to be clear, this is not always an easy process because it is the ego's role to stay in the driver's seat. The ego wants to be first, which is why it will always show up to derail you. It may say, *why bother, it will never work anyway* or it may tell you that you'll never have enough time to pursue your dreams while working full-time. As soon as you get in touch with the soul and become excited about a new venture, the ego will jump in because it wants you to know it exists. The ego is like the toddler who as soon as you answer the phone puts his arms up because he wants to be held. The ego does every little thing to get your attention. And the soul, with its majestic, eternal presence allows it to happen.

The soul has no agenda and all the time in the world. The ego, on the other hand, has a problem with the soul's influence. The ego is temperamental. It wants to be in charge and it will win if you let it. But remember, the ego is not the enemy. While it may create the road-blocks which prevent you from living your best life, it is important to remember that it will warn you when you are about to do some-thing dangerous. The soul is eternal and sees no boundaries. The ego provides the neces-sary boundaries for living in the world. So, es-sentially, what we are saying is that it is a balancing act. You need to work with both your soul and your ego to shine in this life-time.

The importance of balance

When you are not getting in touch with your soul with regularity, and just going about the day to day, you are probably in your auto-mated mind. Ever have the experience of dri-ving to a destination only not to remember the drive at all? You were consciously driving, but you were not present. Your mind was else-where, and this is when the ego has a field day. The ego takes control whenever you are on "automated" because at such times you are oblivious to what is going on inside. And how often are we just going through the motions and not paying attention to our soul needs? If you are not living a purposeful, mindful existence and just moving through life whichever way the wind blows, the ego will be in the driver's seat. And yes, you do need the ego, but you have to prevent it from taking over so your job is to get to know both the soul and the ego very well, and find balance.

While you are living your ego existence, the soul waits patiently. Your readiness to go deeper and connect with it is ironically tied to your inability to keep your life in order. You burn out. You reach a point where the ego is in such a dark place that the soul's emergence is a welcomed sign, and you give up. It is often in our darkest hours that we get in touch. It is hard to believe that something so good can come at the worst times of our lives, but it happens frequently. Such breakthroughs occur during times of grief and unspeakable loss. When the ego can no longer bear the exigencies of life, it gives up like an unruly, frightened child. First it fights hard, but then it fades. And that is surrender. We sometimes also get in touch during the best of times as peak experiences--having a baby, finishing a marathon, falling in love--also opens us up.

The soul can sometimes be more persuasive than the ego, which leads to things like moving a distance from the family to pursue a job, leaving a spouse for a new life, or deciding to move forward with an unexpected pregnancy. It may also come through in unanticipated ways. In 2019, a viral video stunned the world when a murder victim's brother asked to hug the perpetrator of the crime in an open courtroom, and he did. Onlookers were shocked because we are so used to living in a world replete with socially sanctioned behaviors rather than witnessing people doing what their soul is screaming for them to do. We know this. In our hearts, we know it is better to forgive than to harbor anger, even though our minds tell us that we should be angry. But what if we always allowed our hearts lead? If we did, we would make decisions more in line with our true selves.

It is confusing, isn't it? The heart wants what it wants, but the mind holds us back from doing something it perceives as stupid. When a dilemma presents, how *do* we choose? We say listen to your gut, your inner knowing. It is always right. But again, it is a balancing act. So if your inner knowing says you must leave your job, it is correct even if your mind says you need the money. So yes, listen to your soul and plan to leave your job, but don't do it until the time is right. It could take years before you quit, or days, dependent on the circumstances. Also, listening to your soul does not mean you need to make abrupt decisions. Rather, you should be heading in a direction that will bring you peace and happiness. So if we need to balance, why is the soul better than the ego to set you on the right path?

Unlike the ego, the soul is infinite and timeless. Your ego may think it's in charge, but the soul knows that the ego is a human manifestation and the soul lives forever.

Think of your ego as just a tour guide telling you how to navigate Planet Earth during this particular lifetime. It does not understand the deeper part of you. That deeper part is the soul, and once you are connected, you will develop greater awareness that will carry you through your human existence. You may not always consult this inner knowing and may even ignore it for years, but the energy will come back like a good friend who gives you space when you need it. It is always there. And if the soul is so important, you may be wondering why you haven't noticed its presence before, or only noticed during those peak moments we mentioned earlier.

It may help to know that we do not often remember who we are as a soul being nor our past lives or astral journeys, and we certainly don't know what we're doing here, at least not when we first arrive. So we want to emphasize that the source energy that is a part of us, the soul, the piece of us that is who we really are is always there and always accessible. And we know it when we find it. We sometimes find it through meditation, or during a serious illness, or through listening to a spiritual teacher. Sometimes, it comes through when working with the right therapist. We resolve long-standing issues. Or we may discover ourselves through past-life regression or studying our astrological charts. The deeper we go to study ourselves, the more likely we are to find our path and understand ourselves. And this is so important to our development as a human and spirit being. The knowledge is accessible, but our desire to explore varies from person to person. Understanding this and how life works can help you to more successfully navigate it.

To us, the spirit part of ourselves, or the soul, is who we really are, but it can sometimes get buried. This easily happens when life gets busy and there is little time for introspection. But what we really want you to hear is that no matter what is going on in your life right now, you are not broken. You perceive things as a human being, but you are more than that, so much more, and knowing this is the first step

to understanding humanity and your role in
the world.

PERCEPTION

As human beings with a soul and a body, we walk around the planet and engage in the day to day, trying to make sense of the world and live our best lives. And we do things like psychotherapy or meditation in an attempt to make contact with our authentic selves, and although we get glimpses of the soul, there is a lot going on that is of our own making, like the random thoughts that go through our minds every minute, the worries, the fears, and the wishful thinking that is so part of our existence. And we perceive all the information through our own lens so everything that comes into our experience is subjective, and we are usually not gleaning new information because we are picking and choosing what we see and hear. In other words, we tend to embrace the familiar and ignore brand new concepts. It's human nature. But the way we perceive and integrate that information leads us to make decisions for our lives. Think about how important this is.

Every decision you make--from choosing a partner to choosing bathroom tile--is based on information that comes into your experience, the way you perceive it, and the way you weigh positive and negative factors. Your perception then sort of determines your life choices. The best way to understand the concept of perception is to understand the relationship between thoughts and emotions. That is, thoughts can trigger emotions, and emotions can trigger thoughts.

You are what you think about

Neurons talking to one another via electrical impulses create thoughts, so we like to think of thoughts as a form of energy. What happens is that your brain processes memories and decodes information from the environment. As we decode, our minds try to make sense of the world by revisiting the past and thinking about the future. Although we have active thoughts, some of the analytical work is unconscious, which is why you may not understand a burst of anger or why you are suddenly sad without delving deep into your psyche. And while all this is going on, we are rarely present in our own lives.

So think about it: we have tens of thousands of such random thoughts each day and this can cause quite a distraction. Yet, thoughts by themselves are powerless unless we give them meaning, which is why much of its influence depends on perception. In other words, thoughts by themselves do no harm if they have a neutral or positive energy charge, and we can use this to our advantage through the use of affirmations. Affirmations, or positive thoughts, can help you to achieve goals but they will not work unless your heart is in it and unless you take action. Yes, you have to feel as if the good thoughts are true for your desires to materialize. You have to give them meaning. Otherwise, the affirmation will just be another neutral entity that has no effect.

We want the negative thoughts to have zero influence, but we do want to benefit from the positive vibes. Another point is that most of your thoughts are random and fleeting. Have you ever noticed that you may be thinking about one thing, then something interrupts and you are suddenly on another track? Even if there are no interruptions, your mind has a tendency to drift here and there. These thoughts that are mere banter in your head provide you with little direction. They are essentially useless but can do harm if there is a preponderance of negativity and if you believe those negative thoughts.

Negative thinking is what trips us up. It robs us of sleep. It feeds our anxieties. It causes a lot of aggravation and for what? We are talking about thoughts. That's it. These things you take so seriously are no more than ideas. It is your mind run amuck and the strange thing is that you listen to it. Your checking account balance goes below zero. Uh oh. What happened? Did you forget to transfer money from your savings account? Are you living above your means? And what if you lose your job? You only have three months' worth of savings, you think. What if you never get another job and can't pay the rent? Eventually your mind takes you to living on the street when perhaps all that happened is that there was a banking error. That's just one example of negative thinking.

The thousands of negative thoughts you probably have each day can take a toll. Think about it. If you have all of these negative thoughts in your head: *She doesn't like me. Why didn't he call? I'm not sure if I can get the report done on time. I don't know if I'll have the money to pay my bills. I feel a twinge in my tooth. Will I need another root canal?* then you will probably not be very happy. But if you are thinking good thoughts, then you are more likely to be calm, even when things go awry. You know it's true. When you are centered, when you feel your life is going well and you feel good physically, you start the day with enthusiasm and if something does go wrong, you don't let it bother you.

Reaching that place where you feel centered takes some work, but a fast way to change your frame of mind is to simply think good thoughts. Before you read further, it is helpful to buy a notebook with dividers dedicated to the exercises in this book. This way, you will have a central place where all of your work is kept and you can, from time to time, go back and remind yourself about your insights. You may want to divide the book as follows: Good Words, Writing a New Script, Updating, Passions, Intentions, Affirmations and a section devoted to your random thoughts or diary entries. Use and organize your notebook however you like. What is important is that you use the writing processes and keep your work. The first process of using good words seems simple but is extremely powerful and quick to implement.

Use good words

Dr. Masaru Emoto discovered that the element of water reacts to human thought and that beautiful crystals would form in response to positivity, and that similarly, negative thoughts produced less aesthetically pleasing crystal formations. To prove this, Dr. Emoto floated small pieces of paper, each containing positive or negative words and phrases in bodies of water and the results were astounding. His bestselling book *The Hidden Messages in Water* displays images that correlate with the words and phrases. This experiment clearly demonstrates that words are so very powerful.

Now it's your turn. Come up with a list of positive words and write them in your notebook. Look at the list throughout the day. Go one by one, contemplating each word and really feeling it until the list is completed. This is a good process for quickly changing your mindset. We'll give you a list of words that work for us. Feel free to use them:

- Health
- Faith
- Trust
- Love
- Gratitude

So focus on each word above, one at a time, and with the first, envision yourself feeling healthy. What are you doing when you are healthy? How do you feel? What do you look like? How is your energy level? Then go on to faith. What does it feel like to have faith in a higher power and trust in the way your life is unfolding, or trust in other people, and so on? Surely, you love someone. How does that feel? Think of everyone you love, including yourself, and really feel it. Love not only everyone, but every single thing in your environment. Expand on the feeling of love so it surrounds you. And use your imagination. Think of everything you want to do, be or have. You love your desires because the soul vibrates to the energy of love. Love is every-thing around us. Feel it!

And gratitude. What are you grateful for right now? Gratitude goes along with love and has more to do with people than the things you own. You may be grateful for the food on the table or the BMW in your garage, but like everything else in this physical experience, it is temporary. Food will soon turn into energy to fuel your body. And the new car smell and the excitement that goes with it will dissipate. But the soul is real and everlasting so when you think about what is important, you realize that gratitude for the relationships you have will trump your personal possessions.

When contemplating words, you may want to use the ones we suggested, but try to find those that have meaning for you. Some others are Acceptance, Compassion, Hope and Truth. There are many good words in the universe.

Find them. Write them down. Place them in visible areas around your home or use them as screen savers. They will serve as reminders that life is good! You are probably feeling better than when you started reading this chapter. Yes, looking at or hearing good words and learning about positivity can have a profound effect, but it is just the tip of the iceberg.

The importance of thoughts and emotions

Changing your thoughts can be powerful, and perhaps the most enlightening and motivating concept you can embrace is that positive thinking will really change your world. Up until now, you made many decisions--the school you would attend, the profession you are working in, the neighborhood in which you live, how you spend your money, who you hang out with--based on information that came into your experience, how you perceived that information, and the thoughts you think, which leads us to the point: if you don't like the way your life is going, change your thinking. Dr. Wayne Dyer was famous for saying this: Change the way you look at things, and the things you look at change. It's hard to believe, isn't it? The way to change your life is so simple. See things differently. Stop thinking the same negative thoughts over and over again. Of course, the change comes about through our physical efforts, so it is more than just thinking positive thoughts and willing things to go your way. The daily choices we make--big and small--determine the moments we experience and that contributes to the degree of happiness and satisfaction we feel. And the thoughts we think on a daily basis affect those choices, so changing your thinking can help you get to the place you desire. At the same time, we must address emotions. Learning about emotions and how they are interpreted as feelings is critical to resolving the deep conflicts that keep us from making changes in our lives.

First, recognize that emotions are associated with physical form. In other words, the emotions we have are in part created by our physical bodies. You already know this because when a car cuts you off on the highway, your body reacts. Your heart beats faster. You may feel it in the pit of your stomach. But it is not only fear that is felt in the body. Butterflies in the stomach is a phrase used to describe the physical way we feel when we are sexually attracted to someone else. It is that feeling that lets us know, yes, we like him or her.

Emotions are physical, biological, exacting processes. They are your body's reaction to both things going on inside of your body and the outer world, but your feelings are your personal interpretation of the emotions and that makes all the difference. It is why one person can experience running a half marathon as torture and another as the most exhilarating thing they ever did. It is our own unique way of perceiving that makes the difference. Our physical bodies react, but when emotions are felt, our interpretation determines how they are integrated into our daily lives. It is how we perceive an emotion that causes our reactions, our thoughts and our ultimate actions. Understanding this is a game changer. Because your emotions affect your physical body, and are related to how you feel, interpreting them in a more positive way will affect every aspect of your life. You may see some of your stress-related physical ailments improve and you will surely see your mood lift. The heavy weight of emotions that are misinterpreted takes a toll on the mind and the body and it prevents you from getting in touch with your higher self. And while this is great news, there is another element at play that has the potential to make your life even easier, which is that feelings can be derived from other sources.

You now understand that emotions are part of human biology, and are connected to our feelings, but sometimes feelings come from our connection to spirit. Often, the connection results in a positive mood. Some people call it the peace that passeth all understanding when they feel good after a church service, or they report feelings of euphoria when experiencing a new understanding about the spiritual world. It is a high that is hard to reproduce any other way. You suddenly just feel good, at peace, not worried and full of love and compassion. Your energy increases. We call that a high because it does not last. We are human after all and experience a range of feelings. You cannot reach enlightenment and stay there. Rather, you need to experience life--the good with the bad--in order to experience greater growth and appreciation. It is also important to recognize that your feelings are what they are. Sure, working on interpreting emotions will set you on a more positive path, but you should not be expected to feel a certain way. You feel how you feel. Accepting your feelings and experiencing them, but recognizing that they are not the boss of you and are affected by your perception is the first step to living a happier life.

Yes, negative feelings are normal, but they are not desirable, so to minimize them and increase joy all you have to do is experience them, and let go. Feel them and move on. Recognize that the discomfort is just a feeling that gives you information. Sometimes, when feelings are strong, are repetitive or become stuck, it is difficult to do. Alternately, we can delve deep and help resolve them with a process or healing modality, but if they are minor and fleeting, we can just let them go. We get stuck when we hold on tight to a negative feeling. We breathe life into a negative experience when we give it attention. So if you are able, release the negativity on the spot.

To become more aware of your feelings, start small by noticing one feeling at a time. The next time you experience a negative feeling, label the feeling. The feeling is tied to a situation so be clear on how it was triggered. It might have been a phone call that left you feeling defeated and you don't even know what was said to trigger your insecurity. Likely, the trigger was not the phone call but rather, events that happened long ago. Emotions repeat. So, is the circumstance familiar? If it is, you know that something is being dredged up that has nothing to do with your current situation, but of course, it seems to because the thing that happened when you were four doesn't matter anymore. So evaluate the situation and how you are responding. An example of a repeat situation is that you feel left out because your co-workers went to lunch and did not invite you. Is this something that happens often or is this a unique incident? Another example is that you have a fight with your significant other who walks out the door. Maybe he or she is just getting some fresh air to put distance between you but you feel abandoned. Again, is this a theme? Did a parent abandon you? Did an ex break up with you by email?

Trapped emotions become lodged in the body during a traumatic event, and when an experience or thought reminds us of the original situation, the emotion is reignited and often results in a negative feeling. Such an experience is not uncommon and contributes to how we perceive the world. So one way to change your perception is to release these trapped emotions.

It is helpful to drill down to a specific feeling. When you realize you were left out of a group, or that you are alone because your spouse walked out the door, how does that make you feel? You may have more than one feeling. In either instance, you may feel angry. You may also feel lonely. Try to identify the feelings that are most specific to the situation. Are you offended, disappointed, sad or embarrassed? Do you find you often feel this way?

Figuring out why you feel a certain way may be explored in processes and modalities we suggest, but first, there is something you can do right now that will give you an immediate lift that we call resetting. It is a realistic and powerful tool that will move you toward feelings of peace, contentment and joy. While getting to the root of your issues will happen over time, feeling good right now can go a long way to initiate change and see you through difficult experiences. So the next time you're having a rough day, try resetting first.

The process of resetting

Before beginning to use the process, it is important to understand why you are thinking negative thoughts in the first place. Indeed, it may feel like your mind has a life of its own. You think, *how can I think positively when my mind creates negative, sometimes horrific, scenarios?* Well, you already know that there is more going on here than you directing your thoughts. Remember, the mind is often on "automated," where you are simply allowing it to go where it wants. Most of the thoughts you don't want are thoughts that are random in nature. They are often infused with worry or doubt or fear. We equate these thoughts with the Buddhist concept of Monkey Mind. That is, your thoughts are all over the place. If left unchallenged, Monkey Mind will unleash all kinds of negativity. And many outside influences do not help turn them around to the positive. Rather, they may seem to justify your negative thinking. This is because when we are listening to anything we tend to hear only what is familiar to us. So if you start out with negative thoughts, elements from your environment are likely to reinforce them.

The next time your mind goes awry, watch your thoughts. How would they look written down? Do write them down. Or visualize how those thoughts would look on a movie screen. And ask yourself, are these brand new thoughts? Most likely, they are not. In fact, most of your thoughts are re-runs. What to do? Once you have pinpointed the negative thoughts that are troubling you, take a step back and see them objectively. Are they true? Probably not. All of our thoughts are filtered by our own unique perception. But even if they are true, how important are they in perspective? Is this something that will matter one year from now? Once you have determined that certain thoughts are just not relevant, delete them from your mind. In other words, force yourself to stop thinking about the negative ideas. Next, stop whatever you are doing and take a few slow, deep breaths. Then, start a new thread and direct your thoughts with a more positive focus. When you stop negative thoughts and replace them with positive ones, that is what we call resetting. So whenever you are having a bad day, turn your thoughts around. Say to yourself, *okay, I am not feeling great at the moment, but I'm sure things will work out.* Then use the resetting process and move forward as if nothing happened, avoiding the negative self-talk. The worry doesn't change anything, so deliberately change your thinking. It is a quick and easy way to start over.

The resetting technique works in the short term and is particularly effective with thoughts that are not creating major upheaval. While changing negative thoughts to positive ones is critical, it is also important to make changes at a deeper level. Remember, thoughts and emotions are related. All the positivity in the world won't help if you do not understand the role of emotion. We already touched on the idea that emotions are sometimes at the crux of the negative thoughts and that to get past them, you must let them out. Indeed, you need to feel the emotion and see that it is okay to feel bad. The feelings pass. Emotions are a part of the human experience and some will be unpleasant, but it is important not to deny them or run from them by drinking or getting high or using television or sex or food as a distraction. Rather, when they are deeply troubling, we want you to bring them to the forefront by using the process of writing a new script.

The process of writing a new script

Troubling thoughts often involve something going on in our lives that we label a problem. Think about one or more such "problems" and then, grab your notebook and a pen and sit down in a quiet place. What is your most significant problem right now? Once you have targeted a specific situation, deliberately think of a positive thought regarding that problem. Sometimes, the mere act of contemplation will be enough to change the pattern. You may have a worry, but upon thoughtful reflection, realize you neglected to think about a possible resolution, so simply reflecting on that may be enough to change your vantage point. Whatever your circumstance, think of the best possible outcome. Think of multiple positive outcomes. If the thoughts do not involve a future circumstance, but perhaps have to do with something you said that you regret, think of a positive way to move forward. You can think, *everyone makes mistakes and I must just move on.* Or maybe come up with a way to make things right by picking up the phone and calling the person you feel you offended. Maybe they totally understood your intention and have already forgiven you.

This process is not always about making amends and in fact, there is not always a call to action, but sometimes your new positive thought suggests a particular way to move forward. Either way, the new more positive thoughts will move the monkey chatter in a better direction. Yes, Monkey Mind can be changed. After all, the people you know who always seem to be in a good mood likely do think positive thoughts more often than negative ones.

After giving it some thought, is the current situation you contemplated still bothering you? If so, use that. If not, then complete the exercise by putting your attention on another worry. Try to find the problem that is bothering you most. Write down how you feel as well as the thoughts you are thinking. What is upsetting you? Are you thinking about a future outcome? What was your initial thought and where did it lead? For example, an incident may have prompted negative thinking but your mind may have also gone off on a tangent, which provoked additional feelings. This is fine. Write about what is bothering you at this very second. When you write, you are using a different part of the brain than when you are simply thinking so you may be able to get to the root of a problem more easily. And don't try to be positive. Write down everything that is true for you. What are you actually thinking about? Write down your specific thoughts and don't stop writing until you feel there is nothing left for you to say. Write until you are satisfied.

After you are done, you should find that you have identified at least one troubling emotion that is underneath the repetitive thoughts. Are you angry, fearful, jealous or sad? Whatever it is, be with that emotion. How does it feel? It may not feel very good, but by experiencing the emotion for even a short time, you will find that it is only an emotion and will pass. Just close your eyes for a few minutes and feel it. By identifying the emotion, and experiencing it, some of its power is lost. Once you are done working on the emotion, use the process with any other emotion that came up for this particular incident. When you have identified and experienced all of the troubling emotions, then regroup. Take a breath and think about how to move forward by writing down what you want from the situation. The emotions you experienced are all tied to some type of situation, whether it is related to work, a significant other, your health and so forth. Think about that part of your life. What do you want to change, if anything? What do you want your future to look like in this area of your life? For example, if you wrote about a significant other, what do you want the relationship to look like moving forward? If it is a health-related situation, how do you want your body to feel? This may require some thought. You can wait to write this out while you process the problem and then, when you feel ready, come back to this exercise, and write down exactly what you do want. And don't put up any boundaries about what is possible. For example, if your issue is lack of money and you really want to travel, don't make your dreams smaller to accommodate your pocketbook. We want you to write down exactly what you desire. If you were starting from scratch in this area of your life, what would you create?

This writing exercise may reveal that the initial worry has nothing to do with your real hopes and dreams. The initial worry may have sparked another issue deep down in your soul that likely originated a long time ago. The problem with which you started may not matter anymore because the real issue was always something else. Whatever the result, this exercise will help you to change your perspective. And while this process works, it is not something that should be taken lightly nor done and then forgotten. Use it often. Use it every time you are wrestling with one of your problems because if you feel better, but similar issues come up again, you are not done. The reason is because you are working on deep blocks at the subconscious level that stop you from being happy.

Similar problems will surface until you clear those blocks. The important thing is to understand why certain situations repeat. Why is it that every time you call your mother you get into a fight, or every time you visit a certain place, you get scared? Your reactions aren't logical. They are coming from a subconscious memory and the only way to resolve it is to clear it at the subconscious level. Once you do, these repetitive situations will cease.

The process of updating

If you have done the prior exercise, but feel you have not gotten to the root of the problem, you may need to dig deeper to uncover the actual initiation point and understand it. To start, choose a situation that is currently bothering you. You can work on the problem you just wrote about or choose a new focus. Next, we want you to take some time and write in your notebook again. What are the feelings associated with this issue? When was the first time you experienced these feelings? For example, you may remember a time in third grade when you answered a question incorrectly and the entire class laughed at you. Now, you are afraid to speak up at business meetings. And you know why, but you don't know how to get past it. If you cannot figure out the origin, focus on the earliest time you do remember.

Using the above example, the emotion is likely embarrassment. You felt like a fool because you raised your hand vigorously, only to be ridiculed. Go ahead and feel the emotion. Now, you understand what happened and you can still feel the pain of the event when you think about the incident, so we want you to update it. Replace it with what would have been an appropriate response today. Picture yourself sitting in that little third grade seat as you are today and the teacher asks what is five multiplied by two and you say nine and everyone laughs. Now, you may laugh just picturing getting your big self in the little chair, the ludicrous nature of the way that schools are run, and that you actually got such an easy one wrong. But today, you likely realize that you just made a small mistake. After all, you were promoted to fourth grade, right? You just didn't have the answer on the tip of your tongue at the time. It was no big deal. You understand that now because your perception has changed over the years. You are older and wiser and the emotion that was triggered long ago is not you anymore. There is only now, where the you that is present today lives. You think differently and understand life better. If that same incident happened to you now, you would respond another way and would not feel quite so bad. The emotions that are welling up trigger your negative thoughts, but understanding where they come from will help to disempower those emotions. This is not an easy process, and it may take a few tries and some deep thought to figure it out.

Once you understand the emotion, go ahead and update it. Replace it with what you believe would be an appropriate emotion that applies to the current situation. So when your boss reviews your work and finds a mistake, and even if you actually made a multiplication error on a report, you will not be devastated. You may on occasion catch yourself thinking you are stupid like you did in third grade. So it is important to recognize the event as a trigger related to something that happened years ago and that an appropriate emotional response should be much less intense. Today, you may refer to it as a typo or a small mistake, but be aware that the emotional response may be disproportionate if it triggers an earlier event. This is why it is important to recognize the origin. Then you are able to own it and move on. And you can do this because you are thirty-eight, not eight. What you are doing is recognizing the triggering emotion and updating it. You are overriding the old emotion and replacing it with a new response by thinking more appropriate thoughts. Instead of thinking *stupid me*, you are thinking *oh, well. we all make mistakes.* And take it a step further. How do you really feel about the current situation? Maybe your boss is a bit harsh and could have pointed out the error in a less critical manner. Maybe working for her is not working for you.

Perhaps the exercise prompts you to look for a new job, or to seek a transfer or to call Human Resources with a complaint. Or maybe you just stay where you are and recognize your boss as someone who lacks awareness. In any scenario, you should not re-experience the original emotion once you update it. You will just notice it as something that is part of your past and the new experience may be neutral or even positive. You may actually be happy the mistake was discovered before the final report was released!

Sometimes, uncovering the troubling event is the easy part, but how can you update feelings of abandonment or grief or something that is seemingly more serious than making a silly mistake? If the situation involved a death or another kind of separation, the emotions are deeper, and certainly seem appropriate no matter what your age. It then becomes difficult to imagine yourself reacting differently than what you feel now. However, using such an example, the problem is not that the emotions you are experiencing now are not appropriate, but rather, that you didn't feel them at the time, so you get triggered when something similar comes into your environment. Just identifying the feelings may help neutralize the trigger. You can also go back and change the story. Imagine the scenario where instead of being lost or going about your business, you stopped and cried and grieved more. You felt the raw emotions of loss. Rewrite the story so that even though the events occurred, you handled things much differently. When you rewrite a story, it changes everything because what happens to us is largely about the stories we tell. Also, consider what might you have done if the situation happened today, and write about that too.

Why do these processes we just shared work so well? We often bury our emotions. When we face difficult situations, we push through and just go to the next thing. Some of our resistance toward negative emotions is the fear that we will not be able to endure the intensity, but usually, the experience is not as bad as we imagined. Once you are more aware, you will become more resilient and more present, and therefore, less likely to feed your fears. This exercise will help you get to the root of your problems, but if you want to go deeper, other modalities also address blocked emotions such as Reiki, Theta Healing, psychotherapy, tapping, acupuncture, and yoga.

Whether you use our writing exercises or release the trapped emotions another way, the important thing is to recognize the emotional blocks and resolve them.

Changing your perception

We want to reiterate that while thoughts may provoke feelings, feelings similarly provoke thoughts. Sometimes, meditation will open us up and allow feelings to flood forth, and this can be the beginning of understanding and healing the troublesome things we keep inside. Healing in this way will make a positive impact on future thoughts. There is a reciprocal relationship. Work on your thoughts and your feelings will change. Work on your feelings, and your thoughts will change. Both thoughts and feelings play a role in your perception, which is very important. Once you change your perception, your life will change.

We have already provided you with a number of life-changing processes in this chapter and suggested other forms of healing that may be beneficial. Using the processes will help you get started on your journey to change your perception so that you can attract good things into your life, but there is much more to it than this. Changing your perception can significantly help you to feel better about your life. At the same time, making more significant changes requires going within and connecting to a higher power. Doing so will result in lasting growth, but you won't see results overnight. Developing a meditation practice and learning to connect requires repetition and patience. Yet, it is well worth the effort.

The next chapter will show you how to raise your awareness through meditation. Meditation and the awareness that results will help you go deeper to make the best decisions for your life. As you grow, the need for the processes in this chapter will diminish because you will be living in the present and using your inner guidance system. Awareness will help you develop the faith and trust you need to live confidently. Of course, you will sometimes fly off the handle. It's guaranteed. Even after we resolve long-standing emotional conflicts, we are still human beings with feelings and negative thoughts and that will never stop, but the difference is that once you are centered more often, nothing will throw you off balance, and if you do wobble a bit, you will regain your footing really fast. You are starting from where you are, so be patient and don't compare your growth to anyone else's. This is a solo journey. As you become more aware, negative reactions will definitely become less frequent, weaker, last a shorter period of time, and respond quickly to self-correction.

Finally, understand that your view of a situation is totally subjective, but you--as a thoughtful human being--can take a step back and consider a situation differently. When you start thinking more positive thoughts, and know how to handle your emotions, your life will begin to turn in the direction you want, but awareness is truly key to living a joyful life. No matter how much positive psychology you infuse into your life, if you aren't regularly in touch with your soul, your perception can become very negative. The good news is that you can change it through deepening the connection with your soul and the purpose of this book is to show you how.

AWARENESS

Getting to know yourself at the soul level is equated with awareness. Such an awareness has been compared to the act of observing from the inside. And to really get this, it may help to think of the soul as a separate body. Once you think of your soul as a distinct entity, the concept of awareness will make more sense. Generally, when we think about the soul, it seems an ethereal presence, something beyond comprehension, or something you will only experience after you die. You understand the soul conceptually, but you don't think of your soul as a living part of you now. So for purposes of this explanation, we want you to think of yourself as two beings. The French term *un etre vivant* describes it best, which translates to a living being. That's what you know yourself to be. You are alive in the flesh. You are this living creature with not only a body, but a powerful mind of which the ego is a part. And then there is the soul, another being that is always around, always watching, always experiencing and always growing.

The awareness of the soul allows you to override the conscious mind activities because it has a clearer view of any situation. When you are unaware of the soul, there may be a great deal of instability because the ego wants to be seen and heard. You may draw wisdom from the ego, or you could draw error, and you can never really be sure, can you? Your ego is powerful at times, but weak at others and it is not all good. You just never know when your ego will make you miserable. However, we want to reiterate that the ego is not something you need to lose. It's actually helpful. So we want you to think of the conceptualization of both the soul and the ego together as yourself. Your soul has always been with you. Your ego only exists in this lifetime. If you just address your ego problems with processes, it will help a lot, but it will not help you grow at the soul level. To do that, you have to go within.

Awareness: Developing peace of mind

Developing awareness through identification with the soul is the answer to all of your problems. Awareness is experiencing a presence, which may be viewed as an identification with your higher self. A good way to find the awareness we are talking about is through meditation. Simple, but not easy, meditation will get you to that soul experience. We say it is not easy because it takes time to develop a deep practice. It does not happen overnight. Plus, it is not usually easy to sit in silence and just be. It looks easy to just sit down and close your eyes, but when you do, you usually find that sitting is not synonymous with clearing the mind. It just doesn't happen that way. You want to hit your head a few times against a wall to knock those thoughts out, don't you? But while it is normal to be frustrated because you aren't there yet, the truth is you don't actually need to clear your mind to meditate. It is just that you may have to sit and listen to your mind for awhile to get to the good part, at least at the beginning.

The good part comes when you experience deep relaxation and seemingly reconnect with the pure part of yourself. That is, you go deep. You let go and dissociate from the mind. You may sense that the world around you goes away, your feelings disappear, and you just experience the quiet within, or your body may just feel very relaxed as your mind begins to empty. When you find this space, it is always pleasant, and the peace you experience entices you to continue. What does it feel like to experience your soul? Some say that it cannot be explained or described. It has to be experienced. Or they say that if you are doing it properly, you will just know. They are effec-

tively blowing off something we feel should
be addressed. While the whole of the experience perhaps cannot be conveyed with words,
we can certainly have that conversation and
we can definitely tell you what meditation is
not. Did you sit for ten minutes but your heart
is beating quickly and your thoughts are still
racing? If you cannot stop focusing on your
thoughts, are fidgety and waiting until it is
over, or feel angry or frustrated, you're not
there yet. Discerning whether you are doing
it right will in part be communicated by how
your physical body reacts. And it is important
to know that if you sit consistently, you will
get there. We promise. There is nothing very
mysterious about something we see as a
birthright. In other words, you know how to
do this already. You just may not have been
practicing consistently during this lifetime so
it will take some time to remember.

Meditation has been proven to have a relaxing effect on the body and when you engage in the practice, it has beneficial health
effects, such as lowering blood pressure and

reducing stress. So you will experience changes to your physical body. While you are meditating, your heart rate will decrease. You may feel tingly and you will definitely feel more relaxed than when you started. And your respiratory rate will slow. If you are starting with a few minutes a day and nothing is happening, increase the time. It just may take you additional minutes for your mind to settle down. Try sitting for 10 or 15 minutes and notice how you feel afterwards. If it is "working" you probably will notice the physical changes we describe. That is one way you will know that you are actually meditating. So how does it feel to meditate? People describe it in different ways and each experience of meditation is unique, but there are commonalities.

For just a moment, or moments at a time, you may feel a sense of nothingness. It is as if the world around you dissolves and you sense your soul. During such a moment, you do not notice any thoughts and are oblivious to the world around you. Time loses meaning but you retain the awareness of your physical space. Your body may feel good, or you may detach from the body altogether. The connection may last just seconds. It will likely come and go, but those moments will last longer, and increase in intensity, as you deepen your practice and lengthen the time you sit.

At some point, you will find that you are in the space between your thoughts and you are meditating! And you may wonder, is that all there is to it? It seems so simple. Just sit and do nothing. It is, but again, making this connection takes some work. It's like lighting a match. If the matchstick isn't firm enough, or if the matchbook is wet, or if something is off like the angle you are using or the speed at which you move, you won't make the connection and you won't create a fire. But once you light enough matches, it becomes second nature. It's easy then. Scratch just the right way and it ignites every time. So as you practice with greater frequency, you will be able to make the connection more quickly. That is not to say that there will never be times when-- even if you have successfully meditated for years-- you just cannot connect. It happens and it will surely happen to you. Still, if you keep trying, you will be able to access the space more often than not.

Preparing for meditation

First, know that meditation takes practice. Usually, people have a lot of expectations and little patience, but in order to successfully develop a practice, you need to have a lot of patience with no expectations. And you will have to sit or at least be still. You may want to set a timer for five or ten minutes, or even one minute, and just sit, or you may find it more relaxing to not use a timer at all. As you gain experience, it is preferred that you increase to fifteen or twenty minutes or longer. More importantly, do this consistently, like every day. Of course, there is a little more to it than that. Left to your own devices, you would sit and worry about what you are doing next so you have to be thoughtful about what goes on during the time you set aside for meditation. Remember, the goal of meditation is to transcend the mind and just be the presence. Embody this concept by shifting your identity from the ego to the soul so you will be in the right mindset. Planning for your meditation time will also ensure you are in the right frame of mind for a successful experience.

Decide on a good time to meditate. While time of day does not really matter, evening is often a good choice because your energy level is already lower. On the other hand, much depends on your lifestyle. If you live with other human beings, it may be harder to excuse yourself after returning from work at the end of the day. Or you may just want to chill with a glass of wine and Netflix in the evening. Another good time is early morning, before the rush of the day starts. Whether you decide to meditate in the morning or at night or both, or even midday, it does not matter. Being consistent helps, so ideally, meditation will become a part of your routine. Some people meditate with others, such as a spouse or a friend or a meditation group. This is fine, but remember that meditation is an individual experience. You can meditate in the same room as someone else, but ultimately you are alone with yourself once you close your eyes. So there is no real advantage to seeking someone out. At the same time, if you are very extroverted or find commitment difficult, a meditation buddy can keep you honest as you begin to sit regularly.

You may wonder about props or location. Obviously, the quieter, the better. On the other hand, some people find music relaxing. You can try it, but it is not necessary. Similarly, if you like to sit on the floor, a meditation cushion is more comfortable than sitting directly on carpet or wood. Ensure that the space is at a good temperature and that you are wearing comfortable clothing. You may also find that sitting outdoors--perhaps by a brook or just in the sun or on the porch when a cool breeze is blowing--is soothing. Some people like to meditate indoors in front of an altar. Wherever you like is fine, but ideally, it should be a quiet, relaxing environment where you will not be interrupted.

Every day, go to your chosen location at the prescribed time. Try to ensure you will not be disturbed by shutting the ringer on your phone and informing others not to interrupt your practice. Even if you must leave your phone on for emergencies, set it to vibrate so you will not be startled by a ringtone. And if you are thinking you can't or don't want to do all of this, then don't. We are offering suggestions because a consistent practice is desirable, but you can meditate anywhere, anytime and in any environment and you can do so spontaneously and sporadically, without any preparation. While we do encourage routine and repetition, there are no rules. If you are not ready to commit, just meditate when you can, but if you find that a sitting practice is helpful, you might want to incorporate one into your routine.

How to meditate

Once you are in your chosen environment, relax. Sit or recline in a comfortable position. You may have heard that you must sit upright so that your chakras align. This is preferred by many disciplines, but it is unnecessary. That said, you may want to do so and that is perfectly fine too. After you are in position, either close your eyes or select a point of focus such as the floor or a lighted candle. If you choose to meditate with your eyes open, keep your lids relaxed. Notice that you are breathing. Just focus on the breath. Feel your breath. Do not attempt to alter your breathing pattern. Just notice the breath. One way that meditation is taught is to count breaths, but that is up to you. If you do, it will help to interrupt your train of thought, which is a good thing, but this is not necessary, especially if the act of counting bothers you. Just do what feels right. You may be asking, is that it? Yes, that's it. Books have been written about the practice and there is more to talk about, but the act itself is quite simple. And while beginning a meditation practice is a simple thing, it is just the start. The journey that meditation sparks is internal.

Again, simple but not easy, meditation can open up a new world that provides you with comfort and the answers to all of life's woes. But some people feel they cannot do it. Yes, they can sit for a few minutes with their eyes closed, but they say they cannot meditate. Why? They usually explain that they cannot stop the running commentary in their minds long enough to meditate, but that's just not a valid excuse. There are no prizes for stopping thoughts. And did we ever say you had to clear your mind? No, it is part of your own expectation, based on your knowledge and perception of what you think meditation should be. While the act of meditation may result in a clear mind, it will happen naturally, similar to how you fall asleep. You probably know that it is difficult to fall asleep if you are trying too hard, but if you relax and just let your mind go, it will be much easier. Similarly, when you meditate, do not try to stop your thoughts. Just chill and focus on your breath.

Meditation has the goal to create space between your thoughts and to notice the fact that there is space. It is about quieting the mind so thoughts become less frequent. It is about noticing that you are thinking. Yes, meditation is about awareness. Once you notice the thoughts, you are meditating because you are in a different mindset. You are no longer just sitting and thinking and analyzing and ruminating. You are not worrying or judging or comparing. You are not on "automated" anymore. You are noticing that you have thoughts in your head, and are detaching from them. You are feeling the presence. Not unlike the practices from the previous chapter, we want you to continue to see thoughts as nothing more than meaningless banter in your head. The difference between those practices and meditation is that now we want you to stop examining and evaluating your thoughts. We want you to sense the space between your thoughts, and see thoughts as insignificant, no matter what those thoughts are. You may be thinking about baking a cake or about a serial killer who is on the loose, but the content does not matter. Just label the thoughts neutrally as thoughts. To get to that meditative state, you need to stop evaluating and let go, but we know this is not an easy ask.

Your thoughts are likely to interrupt your meditation even more than outside noise. But it is only an interruption if you get caught up in the thoughts and the emotions that go with them. Again, detach and view the thoughts as just thoughts that are void of importance. It may seem difficult, but are you able to read an interesting novel or article on the train where there is noise and movement around you? You just tune it out, right? You probably tune out environmental noise while you are thinking too, but when you are meditating, your thoughts need to become as insignificant as the background noise. Before a meditation session, you will probably choose a quiet space, so you may become annoyed with anyone or anything that disturbs your practice.

But that is life. There will be things in your environment that are distracting: the sound of the door at the house next door, your children in the other room, the television in a neighbor's apartment. You get the picture. You try to be quiet and you find you cannot focus, but we are telling you that you can, because that's the whole point. We want you to sit and deem the background noise as well as your thoughts meaningless. Just keep trying every day. You need to start seeing any interruptions as challenges and not as deal-breakers. Whatever comes into your experience either physically, mentally or emotionally, acknowledge it. This may sound counterintuitive, but it is this awareness that will get you to a place where you can just sit and allow what goes on around you to go on around you, and you will start to get glimpses of the quiet and the space between your thoughts. Revel in these moments when they appear. They will become more and more frequent as you practice.

So sit, notice your thoughts, the sounds you hear, the bodily sensations you feel and also notice the small moments of nothingness that occur. As thoughts come in, or you notice sounds from your environment, or when feelings arise, acknowledge them, but let them vanish into the background. Pay attention to your breathing. That is all you need to do in order to meditate. If you have made an attempt, but feel too tense to meditate, you may be better off postponing for a short time. Get up and do something active first. Then try it again. Have patience. Once you develop a practice, it will be easier to settle down.

As a beginner, feel free to try different methods. It is important to start with the familiar at first so you may want to use music, a mantra or a guided voice meditation. This will help the mind focus on something other than your mind's usual activities. As you focus only on one thing, you train the mind to reduce the brain activities and this gives you control. Then, as you practice, you will notice that you are developing awareness. You are creating space between your thoughts. That space will feel like a wonderful flow of energy that is the real you, and it will seem familiar. You will recognize the energy and from that point forward, you will have a center on which you can visit any time you want.

There are many books written about meditation and we consider this to be one of those, but sometimes, the motivation is not there and we hope by explaining how life works and the power of meditation, you will jump in and try it. And while meditation is probably the most efficient way to make the connection on which we write, it is not the only way to go within. Yes, sitting and getting in touch in silence with your eyes closed is a perfect way to develop awareness, but it is not the only way.

Connecting with your soul

We want to reiterate that even if you have never cultivated a meditation practice, you have already made that inside connection one way or another, or at least have had glimpses of it. Everyone has. Have you ever lost someone close to you? The death of a friend or relative or pet will rattle your world as will experiencing the excitement of winning a big prize or falling in love. In such moments, your sense of time changes. It slows and you are in the moment. Many times, these moments of connection at the soul level come during peak experiences, but more likely they will come while meditating or participating in a religious or spiritual practice. Making breakthroughs in therapy, or experiencing synchronicities or connecting with another person deeply also helps to open up a pathway to the soul. And recovering from a long illness, beating cancer, or living through any physical challenge usually provides moments of spiritual depth.

These experiences of elation or despair as well as the quiet moments in between make up a life that is replete with connections to the soul. If you are very young or have not faced many hardships, you may have experienced only fleeting moments of connection. That everyone has been there on some level proves that we can all get there. Everyone has already experienced the connection with the inner self to some degree, but these tiny moments are likely never acknowledged. So what we are suggesting is the creation of an environment in which connecting becomes more frequent, which will increase its potency. Doing so will rock your world because getting in touch with that part of yourself on a regular basis--developing awareness--changes everything.

Mindfulness

Awareness, or sensing the presence, may also be achieved through simply being in the present moment. It can be a very powerful experience and it will give you many of the same insights as meditation. And it may be a good place to start, especially if you are resisting a sitting practice. Of course, engaging in both practices is ideal. Meditation allows you to go deep and find yourself and mindfulness opens awareness and insights as you go about your day, enhancing your positive experiences and making some of the more unpleasant ones a little more tolerable. Think about it. Most of us are multitasking. Our minds wander. We watch television but find that we are looking at our phones so much that we cannot keep track of a plotline written at a third-grade level. Yet, we are intrigued when we physically walk through a field of colorful autumn leaves or we become excited by an impending snowstorm. Real life is never boring, so when you stay with whatever you are doing and avoid distraction, you are being mindful. Even if you watch a television show, but instead of allowing your mind to wander, you laser into it, you are being mindful. You feel you are a part of it. You empathize with the characters. You are thinking of nothing else. Your mind doesn't wander when you are riveted. And if you cannot do that with the television program you are watching, maybe you are bored and need to find a new show.

Mindfulness can happen anywhere and at any time. There are no specific "mindful" activities nor are there activities that preclude the ability to be in the present moment. It is not what you do that matters; it is how you do it. But even when we are trying to be mindful by getting out in nature or some such thing, we are easily distracted either by our company or our thoughts. You may be engaged in a great conversation, or solving the world's problems in your mind, but you are no longer focusing on experiencing nature with all of your senses. This does not necessarily create a bad experience, but you are not being mindful of the thing you intended to be mindful about. On a daily basis, your life is filled with moments when you are not totally present. How many times has your mind wandered while reading this paragraph? Did you have to read parts of it over again because you were thinking about the pancakes you just put in the microwave or the dog you let out in the yard a few minutes ago? Most of us are multitasking or even if we try to devote our time to one task, we are unable to keep our attention on that task for very long.

Mindfulness is using all of your senses while engaging in an activity. To demonstrate this, Jon Kabat-Zinn, a pioneer in the mindfulness movement, asks his students to eat a single raisin but to make sure to experience its smell, taste, texture and so forth. By using all of the senses during the exercise, his students get a sense of what it is like to be in the moment. It also makes one aware that we aren't usually paying attention because the exercise feels totally different than what normally happens. Usually, we would not eat one raisin at a time, nor would we be so focused on the experience. Rather, we would mindlessly chew a few raisins and pay little attention to how eating affects the senses. This type of exercise teaches the art of presence.

Mindfulness is really all about the awareness of the soul, fully living in the present moment, and not allowing the ego to intrude. It is not about stopping thoughts, but rather, it is about experiencing the presence or using thought to solve a problem or accessing the space to create something new. It is also about being fully-engaged with life. It is about showing up and being the best you can be by focusing on what is in front of you or what is happening now. So if you are sitting and solving a crossword puzzle while thinking of nothing else, you are being mindful. If you are having a conversation, looking into the other person's eyes and listening to what they are saying, you are being mindful. Whenever you focus attention on what you are doing whether it is viewing a painting at an art gallery or running a marathon or making love or swimming in the ocean—and are not being distracted by random thoughts—you are being mindful. And this mindfulness is not just an activity to do on occasion. It is, for as much as you are able to do it, a way to live your life.

Making the connection a part of your life

Achieving awareness is at the crux of our philosophy, which is that connecting with your inner knowing is vital for a fulfilling life. By practicing meditation and mindfulness, you will be able to connect with the energy more often and not get derailed by your ego.

The connection helps you make decisions and feel better about your life. If you don't have a meditation practice, and are not living mindfully, you may connect from time to time, but you have not synthesized the experience. It is not conscious. Rather, such rare moments are fleeting and though they may occasionally be life-changing, it is not the same as being in the space most of the time.

Additionally, we are more than our souls. We each have a human body, and meditation has a powerful effect on it, which is why many medical professionals are on board with the practice. Reducing stress through meditation and mindfulness can have a significant and positive impact on your physical health. Meditation also has profound spiritual capabilities, which is why it is at the center of many healing modalities. It is a door to your higher self. It does take a bit of practice to connect, but once you do, you will have greater clarity about your life, and you will become more intuitive. If you rely on that intuition, you will be following the only guidance you will ever need. And once you know how to connect, you will be able to do it anytime and anywhere. And if you are present in your life for much of the time, the access to your inner world will be automatic. You will not have to do anything. It will be how you live. But when you find that you are distracted by your ego, you will just need to take a breath and reset.

The reason why it is so important to meditate routinely is so that your connection will deepen and you will find that you are in a state of awareness more frequently. Just like lighting a match, the more you do it, the easier it becomes to get into that space. You will be able to access this part of you instantly and sometimes get spontaneous answers to the questions you want to resolve. Do you know someone who lives life through their gut and never thinks things through? If they are really connecting within, and not just being reactionary, they are tapping into their inner knowing. But that is not the only benefit of establishing this connection. If you consistently go within, you will be more confident about your choices and know just what to say or do in any situation. You will know what is right for you. You will recognize the familiarity of being in that space, you will feel more loving, have more gratitude and be more accepting and this will lead to greater happiness because this is the true nature of your being.

It's a good idea to approach your meditation periods with a question in mind as your higher self may have an answer for you. Don't force an answer. Don't even think about the question while you sit. Bring no expectations to the session. Just be. You will start to notice that as you meditate more and more, your questions will get answered and you will start to connect with your inner knowing. All too often, we rely on the opinions of others, especially when they have advanced degrees in a subject area, but they do not necessarily know what is best for us. Only you know what is best for you. And that is not to say that you should not look outside for information regarding particular quandaries. Of course, you will probably want to consult experts or read journal articles to make the best decisions for your life, but the difference is that you own the decision. You listen to advice and check within, and then say to yourself, yes, that feels right or you may say, no, it doesn't work for you. And then you go from there.

Connecting with source energy through meditation and mindfulness will make you feel better within your mind, body and soul. That is what we are talking about. You can change everything by forging a connection with yourself. And everybody can do this. Everybody does this to some extent. We just want you to know how important and life-changing the deepening of this connection can be.

LOVE

If you have read the first four chapters and are doing the exercises and meditating and being mindful, you are probably feeling better right now, but we do want to address a very important component in your life, which is love. When you hear the word "love," what do you think about? While of course we love our parents and children and friends and pets, the term often conjures romantic images. Stories like *Cinderella* or *Romeo and Juliet* pop into our minds. They are love stories. We all want the starring role in one of those, but what if we told you that the magnificence of the beloved is an illusion? We are not saying that your love for a particular person is not real, but we do want you to realize that the feelings you have for the object of your affection is based on your perception. Your boyfriend or girlfriend may have an almost angelic presence and is perfect in your eyes, but who they are from your vantage point is based on how you see them. Can you begin to see the fallacy of being in love? You are in love with the fantasy version of the person you desire.

That is, you excuse a human being for whom you are very fond from all their shortcomings. You see them as larger than life, superior to others and yes, you love them in the real sense of the word too. You care for them. You care what happens to them. You hurt when they are hurting and are happy when they are happy. And while real love does include this alignment where you experience empathy, too much empathy isn't good either. You do need to know where the other person ends and you begin. You need boundaries in order to develop your fully human-spirit self. All of this holds true for your significant others or when you feel you are "falling in love," but we also have these experiences--though to a lesser extent--with other important people in our lives. So the real goal is not to fall in love with one individual who is perfect for you because that is an illusion, but rather to foster unconditional love for all people. And the ask is much easier because being in love--the kind of love that love stories are made of--is unsustainable. It is a lot easier to decide to actively and unconditionally love all human beings than to try to find one person with whom you develop an exclusive connection.

So let's say we decide that we will love others just for being human. In an ideal universe, there would be only love, but even in our best human relationships, there will be disagreements. Good relationships may be difficult at times and bad relationships may present serious challenges. So if we feel miserable when we are with another person, why bother with the relationship? Many people do end marriages or leave jobs because they can no longer tolerate being in relationship with a particular person. Author Jean-Paul Sartre wrote the infamous work *No Exit* where the conclusion is *hell is other people.* Sometimes, it feels that way. After all, aren't most of your negative feelings triggered by another individual? But as human beings, we are social animals and there is yet another reason to engage with people, even if we don't like them all the time. It is one way that the soul grows. So while getting along with others can sometimes be daunting, and the world at times seems more divided than united, there are things to keep in mind.

One is that total bliss is just an impossibility, and it is good for the soul to be challenged. It is through disagreement that we end up with greater understanding, and it is often our lack of attention that causes misunderstandings. So listen to what people are saying. Like you, they are doing the best that they can to live their lives. Most people are good and altruistic, but we communicate differently and we perceive each other in different ways because everyone is unique. That is what makes the world go round. So celebrate differences, but seek to understand. Every relationship you foster, including relationships with your parents, your co-workers and your friends is of your own making.

Whenever you are judging or in conflict with others, know that the reason you feel bad is because you are separated from the source energy to which we are all attached. When we refer to source energy, we mean God or the universe or whatever you want to call it. We use these terms interchangeably but they all mean the same thing, which is an indescribable living, intelligent energy. The more you are connected, the less conflict and the more joy you will experience. This is because when you are connected, you are in the present moment. You are listening to other people rather than the criticisms in your head, so your thought patterns and conditioned beliefs disappear. And then you begin to see the divinity in others. You feel empathy for the person you are with. You are more likely to accept their behavior or able to confront another person if their behavior is hurtful. Above all, you can access your honesty because your presence allows you to let go of the identification with the ego. It is simple, but it is not always easy to achieve harmony. And sometimes you will not want to mend a relationship. But for the people you choose to keep in your life for the long haul, things will work out if you continue on the path. If you are meditating and creating space for a change of heart, your mind will follow, and your relationships will improve.

Detach: Focus only on your own life path

It may seem counterintuitive, but emotional distancing, or detaching, can enhance your close relationships. This is because too much closeness can result in a desire to manipulate or control the other person. Sometimes, you may think that if only a particular significant person in your life would only do a particular thing you want them to do, you would be really happy. This is your first clue that your ego is getting into the act. Someone else will never make you happy through their actions. For example, you want your daughter to fill out college applications when she wants to take a gap year or maybe you want your spouse to ask his boss for a raise but he thinks that will make things worse, or you want your mother to see a doctor about a worrisome symptom when she prefers to avoid medical intervention altogether. But you don't know that your advice is really the right thing for them.

It is tempting to try to change someone else's world or to provide advice or to urge a certain action when it is not any of your business. You think you know what is best for your mother or brother or son or daughter, but do you really? Yes, we are all connected in some way, and you may love the people in your life very much, but they are here to do their lives and so should you. That is, focus on your own path, not someone else's. You may think it might be nice for your son to land the job he just applied for, but you don't know that. Maybe the universe will say no to that because there is a better job coming in three or six months. You may have your hopes set on some outcome for someone else, so we are asking you not to do that. We want you to detach. And yes, this goes for significant others too!

Remember in school when you'd take a test and the teacher declared that you should keep your eyes on your own paper? The teacher said this to everyone because she knew some people would cheat. Now, imagine rows of individuals sitting at desks with a sheet of paper in front of them. The papers represent their lives. The takeaway is that you need to focus on your own paper and stop looking at someone else's. You may want to be helpful, but it's just not right. And you need to put up boundaries for yourself too. No one else should be looking at your paper either. We all have that inner guidance system. Let's use it!

We know it is not easy to detach from

someone else when you feel close, but too much caring will not only make you miserable, and cause you to feel attached to outcomes regarding situations that do not even affect you, it will hinder the relationships you care most about. So have faith in the universe and trust in the individuals you want to help. They can navigate their own lives, even though you think you know what's best for them. Conversely, you may be troubled by a relationship that is not close nor loving. It may be a boss or an ex-girlfriend or a relative that really irks you. They may have done something to you that you perceive as unfair or unkind, and you may have even gotten a fair number of people to agree with you. Yes, we get it. Sometimes, people act in negative ways and it is hard to see the good in them. Whether you are in love with the individual pushing your buttons, or you detest them right now, just stop. No one can make you feel a certain way. Again, feelings are complex and tied to thoughts. If you are obsessed with another's actions or lack of it, you are thinking about them. A lot. Too much. So use the techniques we provide in Chapter Three to gain clarity, and then detach. Know that the person is not doing anything to you. You are, by thinking about them. It may be difficult, but the process of detaching from either someone you love or despise will become easier as you begin to know yourself better and connect with a higher power. You will then develop the faith and trust you need to let go of the expectations of other people and come to love and respect each person for who they truly are.

Love yourself first

To improve your relationships, you will also have to change the relationship with yourself. We have all heard about self-love and the notion that you have to love yourself before you can love anybody else. The phrase in fact is almost cliché. And while we are jumping on the bandwagon, we don't want you to just nod in agreement. We want you to understand the magnitude of self-love and how powerful you will become when you really love yourself. Self-love is hard to define, but we can tell you what it is not. It is not conceit or entitlement. If you put yourself in high esteem at the expense of others, there is a lack of self-love, not too much. You can never love yourself too much because the love you feel for yourself spills out into your life and touches other people. It spills out into your life just like the ocean seeps into the crevices of our bays and rivers. Love is everywhere. It is not something that can be selfishly contained. Self-love is not selfish. It is an experience of love. So what is love anyway?

Universal, basic concepts like love are hard to explain. There are no words that adequately describe the fuel of the universe. But to try to convey it a little better, think of what you feel for your children, your pets and your best friend. You feel a desire to nurture and care for them. That's love. And you can do that for yourself too. Self-love always comes from strength, connected to source and infused with joy and goodwill. It is self-acceptance with gratitude and the knowledge of your own vulnerability. It is your understanding that you are one of many, not worth more nor less. Another way to look at it is to think of love as a verb. It is something you actively do.

Loving yourself means being kind to yourself all the time. We are often most critical of our own actions, but when you do something you regret, think about what you would say to a good friend if she did that same thing. Would you be kind, and careful not make her feel worse because you care about her? Of course you would, and you can do that for yourself. You can love yourself by trusting your intuition and your experience. Getting in touch with your higher self through meditation and mindfulness is key to self-love. When you do this, you flip the switch, and the egocentric persona shatters and "it's all about me" becomes "I am all there is."

It is your self-worth, your understanding that your word is law in the universe and that you are the most important thing there is that must be understood because without you, there would be nothing, at least not in your personal experience. But everyone else in the world has this same sense of self-importance and deserves the same love as you do. Do you get it? It is why you cannot love anyone else until you love yourself because you are all there is. You are the center of your universe and you have endless love to give. When you are "in love," you are seeing that other person through God's eyes, but if you want to own that person, it is your ego desire, and not love. So falling in love is not exactly what you thought it was, but loving is absolutely something accessible and it all starts with loving yourself.

DEATH

So you are living your life without the angst and weathering the storms rather gracefully, and feeling your emotions and experiencing the relaxing effects of meditation and falling in love with the world, and suddenly a new thought pops into your head: *I am going to die* and *everyone is going to die.* Yes, it's true. And it is the one thought that can easily burst your happiness bubble. Just when you have every-thing you want, and life is going great, you fear losing it all. And you want to hold onto every precious moment because you know this life is temporary. And at the same time, you may think, *what's the point? Time is fleeting. Before you know it, I will be living the final days of my life.* Well, that's depressing. Many people do think about this, and to combat these fears, they try to extend their mortal lives by living as healthfully as possible. After all, if you feel you have thirty more years to go, rather than fifteen, it feels much better. Death is further away. A good idea just to ensure your own bodily comfort, living a healthy lifestyle will not resolve the death thought because even if you do live a long time in a healthy body, you will eventually be closer to death, and the fear doesn't cease anyway.

What you think you really want is to live forever, but do you really? You probably don't want to literally live forever. You just don't want this fear of dying to have a grip on you. So think about it. Why are you so attached to the notion that dying is a terrible thing? We would like to say that the reason for the attachment is obvious, but it is actually not so obvious. The death thought is your ego talking, and it generates emotions, which in turn prompts you to think more thoughts about dying, and so the fear is nothing more than that. Don't think of it as a human condition that cannot be resolved, or some cosmic joke on mankind. Death is not larger than your ego. Indeed, the resistance to dying is just your ego fighting for its life because in order to exist, it must maintain a distinct identity. So death is not what you think it is. You as a spiritual being will never die. It is only the body and the ego that dissolves. The essence of you, or who you really are, continues on. So death is not something to be feared. And as you may already know, there are worse things.

Losing someone you love is a bit harder to accept than your own demise. You don't know what death will be like, but you do know what life will be like without your significant other, or a child or a parent. At least you think you do. When you die, your ego no longer exists and your energy will be free of the bodily restrictions, so it is all good, but when you lose someone on the earth plane, you will in all your humanity miss that person terribly. But think about it. They are not really gone because their spirit continues to exist. It is your ego that has a difficult time accepting this, and that is because you will no longer see, hear or touch the person ever again, and you want that so badly.

The finality of death is alarming. It shocks us first into a sense that this cannot be, that it is not happening, and then perhaps anger and anguish, and a roller coaster of emotions flood forth. Human emotion is raw and part of who we are. The shock is equated with the realization that life is an illusion in some way. We have people in our lives that are always there for us, whom we love, and who we never want to be without, but death can take anyone away at any moment. So the circle of people in our lives we consider a permanent state is really just part of how we perceive our lives, even though deep down, we know that human life is fragile. We know our parents are supposed to die before us, and that we are supposed to die before our children, but sometimes, life doesn't unfold as expected and anyone can die at any moment. The miracle in fact is that, with so many things that can go wrong, we live.

Remember, we are physical beings and spiritual beings combined and only living in this time and space for a purpose, but life is not always easy and in fact, if your life were all peaches and cream, you would not be reading this book trying to make yourself feel better and if you selected this book because you are grieving, and just skipped to this part, we urge you to read the book from the beginning. The tools are all here. No, your deceased loved one is never coming back in the flesh, and it *does* matter, but understanding who you really are and getting in touch with the essential part of you will bring an understanding that goes beyond human emotion and will help you through the grieving process.

We also want you to really understand that grief is actually all about you and not the other person. We want to believe that it is about the person who died, how great they were, and how much they will be missed. When someone dies we commiserate with others and the rituals of the western world are attached to the persona of the deceased. If we did not show emotion, or actually celebrated rather than accept sympathetic offerings, it would be a horrific denial of what we have come to see humanity to be. In other words, society expects us to show our suffering and how much we care. And it would seem selfish to acknowledge that someone else's death is about you and not about them. But really, if you think about it, it is about you. We are so aligned with our egos, it is sometimes hard to see the truth. If it were about the person who died, you would in fact be celebrating their transition, but what you are really grieving is the part of you that was intertwined with their human life. Your life will change. It is a loss for you, not them.

As time goes on, we never forget our deceased loved ones, and never stop missing them, but their presence fades to some extent and our acceptance of the situation increases.

Many people report being able to sense their presence from time to time. Knowing that their spirit is still alive, and that we will connect with them someday in a nonphysical form, helps to put things into perspective. Moving forward after insurmountable loss is very difficult, but it is possible to laugh again, to feel good again, to connect with our best selves and to create a new chapter without our cherished friends and relatives. We are able to hold onto memories of our loved ones, which helps to keep them alive in our hearts while we enjoy our human experience. If you have just lost someone close, perhaps you cannot imagine what we're saying is true, but it is possible when you are in touch with your soul.

Hopefully, you have at least begun to see that death is just another thought and it is your ego thrashing about and having a fit because it is fighting for its life. Everything is okay in this present moment. You are not dying at this particular point in time. You are safe. You are here. You are just reading a book. If you are thinking about your own mortality or someone else's, and that is upsetting you, it is because you haven't yet integrated that the concept is what is making you unhappy. So if the fear of death really has a hold on you, relax. Have patience. It will take time to integrate this new way of looking at death because you have feared the idea of dying so much all of your life. Take a step back and see your thoughts as neutral. Remember, thoughts are meaningless. And recondition your thinking so you see death as just a doorway to another world, just as birth is a doorway into this one. And it is inevitable.

Think of life and death as a roller coaster ride. It all starts when you wait in line. You're excited for the ride, but you do not know how it will feel, and you don't know if perhaps something will break or whether you will feel sick or a number of other things. You are dealing with uncertainty. You kind of know what will happen, but you just don't know for sure. You enjoy the ride for the most part, but there are some scary moments. The ride does not go on forever. It ends at some point, and then you may choose to wait on line again. And if you believe in reincarnation, that is a good analogy for what happens. You go on the ride of life with all its ups and downs, and then you keep repeating.

No matter what your beliefs are about the afterlife, your physical body will at some point cease to function. Accept this. But while life as you know it will stop, your consciousness will live on. Consciousness is energy and cannot be destroyed, and the fact that energy cannot be destroyed is part of scientific law. Don't forget, you were this consciousness before you were born. You came into a human body in order to grow your consciousness. But the thing of it is that you do live forever. It is the premise on which Christianity is based. It is this promise on which most organized religion and spiritual disciplines agree. We do live forever. Our souls go on and our souls know this. The soul, the piece that is really you, is invisible and indescribable. We equate it with energy. This spirit energy continually charges itself with love and you are more and more becoming this love energy. As the love energy evolves, you may be able to let go of the idea of fear, attachment and judgment and the illusion of separation from source energy. As you move away from these less desirable ideas, and move toward love, you become more like God. When you die, no matter how much of your ego you shed during your life as a human being, you will become part of the universe again.

Thinking about this is one thing, but really believing that you go on forever is another. You may say, okay, you get it, but you still don't want to die and we will tell you it is a fear, and you will say, *so what? I still don't want to die.* So we would tell you, we understand. It is human nature not to want to die. There is a fear of ceasing to exist, but again, it is your physical body and your ego that dies, not who you really are. And if you really want to stop the fear of death, we will give you the same advice as we did when we told you how to deal with your random thoughts. The most important thing you can do when you fear death or miss a departed loved one is to meditate. Sit, breathe and be with the presence. Embrace everything that comes with that experience. This is the part that will live forever. And when you feel comfortable in your own skin, and you know who you really are, you may still have some human fears, but you will have a peace and a confidence about life. The goal is to choose unconditional love every time and let go of the fear. Recognize the fear for what it is: your ego.

And remember, we are what we think about. If we continually think about our impending doom, we will be fearful, but if we don't think about death, we can continue on with our fabulous lives. And the understanding of this comes best at a visceral level. No amount of rationalization will ever come close to what you experience when you are meditating. You become one with the universe. You are in touch with the part of you that intuitively knows it lives forever. So the more you get in touch with this part of yourself--yes, we are saying this a lot because it is the key to everything--the better you will be about accepting the inevitability of death.

FLOW MANIFESTING

You now understand how to forge a deep connection with yourself, you are tapping into an inner knowing of which intuition is a part, and you are carefully examining your thoughts and emotions. If you have been engaging in these practices for some time, you are starting to notice that you are calmer and making better choices. You are experiencing the presence more frequently and not attached to your thoughts. You realize that thoughts are just thoughts and do not have to run your life. You are able to experience your life rather than move from one thing to another. You are also happier. You are doing the things you only previously imagined because you have more confidence and realize that you can fulfill your desires. Once you have that connection, you know that you are more than the flesh and bones that make up your body. There is a world out there, and while you will dissolve into the other world after you are finished with this lifetime and the body no longer exists, you want this experience to have meaning. And perhaps you think there is something more. There is.

We each come into the world at different levels of spiritual understanding and no matter where you are in your spiritual journey, the way to change is to go deeper, to get to the next level, to grow. As your soul grows, you will tap into that something more that excites you and is beyond anything you will experience by just living your daily human existence. No matter where you begin you can always go deeper and always get more connected. If you have gotten this far in the book and are walking the walk, you are not seeing these concepts for the first time and are already in a higher state of consciousness than the majority, but it may surprise you that well over half of the world's population is in a state of being where they merely follow, conform and fit in. Others have come into the world questioning what they see around them. They question--sometimes at an early age--where we go after we die or they are curious about the occult. They want to know more about what they have been told to believe about the world. They often feel like misfits and sometimes have a unique path. While some stay at this level of questioning, others continue the journey.

In the spiritual state of seeking where you already are aware that there is something more, there is greater contentment. You may fall back into old patterns or ways of thinking at times, but you have come so far on your spiritual journey that there is no turning back. You cannot unsee what you already know. You have found that bright light inside and you continue to grow your consciousness. You draw on your intuition to make choices. Your desire for knowledge is insatiable. You know there is something more and you know you will never find it because the growth is in the seeking. As you continue to grow in this higher state of consciousness, you begin to explore things about yourself you never considered previously. You begin to wonder how you can live life on this planet in a meaningful way. Meaning becomes central to your experience. But remember, the spiritual state is vast.

When you begin, you are questioning, but as you ease into your inner knowing, your state of being changes. You wake up and see that living in the present moment is the only reality you want. Sure, you will still use your mind, but you do not want to go back to being on "automated." Rather, you use your mind to verbally connect with others, to make decisions as situations arise, and to plan and put things you want into motion. When you reach a higher level of consciousness, you do not get caught up in your negative emotions or react with anger quite so much, but no matter where you are, you will never completely get rid of the ego. And remember, developing this awareness is a process, not an event. It happens over time.

If you keep growing in the spiritual state, and dig deep, you want to play with life. Things are lighter because you are not filled with angst and chasing thought forms in your head. You now have room to create and you might come up with a purpose or a passion, or find out what you are here to do or what you want to do. At this point, you may want to consult a counselor, an astrologer or a coach, but you may be able to discern your calling without seeking any outside support. That is, you just know. If you are meditating, and getting in touch, you will find your north star one way or another.

The expression "north star" is equated with finding your purpose in life or what you are here to accomplish. Sometimes, you don't have to find it because it finds you. A stray dog may wander into your home and you become obsessed with dogs and become a veterinarian or dog trainer or dog sitter. Or you happen to get a university brochure in the mail by accident and end up taking a course that leads you in a different direction. Look for these synchronicities. They're all around. You just have to notice them. And while you will likely see signs along the way, at this very moment, you may not know what you want to do with your life nor do you ever need to discover a single purpose. We will help you explore your passions with the exercises below, but first, we want to introduce the concept of Flow Manifesting. After all, that is why you bought this book, right? And you are eager and ready to begin, but what if we told you that you were already doing it?

By the time you are reading this section, you should be in the final stretch of integrating the method. This is because to engage in Flow Manifesting, you first need to understand who you are as a soul and a human being and then you will need to practice emotional hygiene by clearing out much of the negative reactivity we all experience. If you have gone through the processes we provide in the book and you are practicing mindfulness and meditation, you are already engaged in the process. But if you picked up this book and gravitated to this section first, you will need to start from the beginning, including our Dear Reader letters, because much of what you need to know about Flow Manifesting is there. We realize it takes some time to integrate the method, and you will fluctuate from being in your head to being aware, but if you start from where you are, you can only improve and become centered at least most of the time, and then and only then will you begin to experience what we call Flow Manifesting.

But there is more to it than that. The rest of this chapter will take things from there. So now, you are centered more often and finding meaning and experiencing more joy and peace. You are in the right mindset to truly discover your passions and essentially, you are in sync with the universe. You are making things happen. But it gets better. You can engage in powerful exercises to take things to the next level through knowing what you want, setting an intention to get it and using tools and techniques to get you to where you really want to be.

Flow Manifesting Step #1: Discover your passions

Many of us think we have to choose just one thing on which to focus our lives. You may be asking what you are meant to do. But the answer is not always simple. And there is not always a single answer. You may embrace multiple interests and never quite get set on one path. And while that is perfectly fine, it is important to find at least one thing you are passionate about. Why? Passion is a force that will push you to explore your interests and help you to grow. It is a reason to wake up each morning. It makes life richer and more exciting, and it creates joy. Although waiting for things to come into your experience can work, when you find something you really love to do, it makes perfect sense to pursue it. And it does not matter how old you are. You can discover a new passion during any stage of life. And it need not be your central focus. We want you to find passion in multiple aspects of your life. You may also refer to these things as likes or desires, but don't include anything you can take or leave. A passion is something you definitely love, and not something you have to think about. It is a definite *hell yeah* and never a maybe.

So think about what excites you. It may be trying a recipe or meeting someone new. You may get a thrill while attending a concert with a hundred thousand other fans or it may be a lone walk on the beach on a sunny day. Sometimes we think about something exciting and want to make it happen. We think about how to bring a thing or a situation we want into reality. But don't get hung up on how things are going to unfold. Just think about what you want and not on how life will play out. Focus on what you truly desire, but be careful. Sometimes we want to attract things into our lives because we are told to want them. Remember the ego and how it differs from the soul? The ego may want the big house only to be able to show it off. The ego isn't necessarily concerned about the hours of maintenance the home requires. Even with hired help, a large house is a responsibility and a known time suck, so when you are thinking you would rather be photographing a sunset than looking at kitchen cabinets, know that your soul is calling. And if you want the mansion, that's okay as long as that is your true desire and not something put into your head by the larger society. Sometimes, we just don't know where our true passions lie.

Discerning your passions is important because if you want the best experiences to come into your life, it is a whole lot easier if you know what those are. This is because while you may be in sync with your highest good, and attract positive things, intention is an important part of manifesting and makes the process much more powerful. So do you know what you want? We ask this not to elicit a response like, I want to be a fireman or the CEO of a large corporation, because that is not your whole life. Your goals should not be focused on one dimension of your life. Even if you have a high-powered career or a calling to something you are passionate about, you should have other aspirations, such as finding a significant other or strengthening a current relationship, traveling to a certain desirable locale, finding a new hobby, going back to school, or just finding new friends. Other personal goals may be to have a family or to move to a different location or adopt a kitten. There are things that you certainly want and the thoughts are going through your mind here and there, but we want you to be deliberate now as you focus on the things you truly desire.

If you are having trouble uncovering your passions, think back to when you were a small child. Use whatever memory comes up for you. Childhood was a time when you were open to life, but with each year you grew older, the ego grew too. As we age, we often let go of the best part of ourselves to dive into the world of ego and forget about our true essence, the energy consciousness within us that was so alive during childhood. We desensitize ourselves from our soul traits. We often forget about the light and the power within and leave imagination where we think it belongs: in childhood. But if we can remember what we wanted to do during our early years, it just might culminate in a new zest for life.

Did you paint or draw or did you love physical play outdoors? If you have a job working for a large corporation, lost in the hierarchical structure, wouldn't you rather be a ballet dancer or a basketball player or front a rock band? Of course, you think, who me? You could never quit your day job and do something crazy. Relax. That's not how it works. We don't subscribe to the do what you love and the money will follow philosophy, at least not without considering the practicalities. We don't believe that if you just quit your job and hope for the job of your dreams, it will come, but we do believe that you are a powerful creator and that you can create the life you want, even if your dream is to become a famous musician! In the end, you may not be in the role you imagined, but as you move toward your passions and experience a shift in consciousness, you will surely manifest the career you were meant to have. And perhaps the best part is that you will enjoy the journey, even if you never reach a specific destination.

Another thing to consider is that you still might enjoy your day job and the lifestyle it affords, even if the job is not a passion. You can go to the ballet after work, play basketball on the weekends or start a garage band in your free time, but if that is not fulfilling, you can certainly take it to the next level. Ideally, you will be passionate about your primary line of work, but there may be practical reasons to keep an unsatisfying career path going. Maybe the field is right, but you are working in the wrong company or with the wrong people. Think about what drew you to that mediocre job in the first place. Maybe a passion is lurking under the discontent, or maybe the job creates the earning power or perks you need to make a passion materialize.

Flow manifesting may be used to explore vocational passions, but again, it applies to the enhancement of all of your life situations, including relationships. When you are in touch with your inner world and are aligned with the universe, and you take steps toward your greatest good by understanding your true desires, you are manifesting through being in the flow. Synchronicities will occur. You will begin to see what you imagine materialize in real life. When you look back after several years of being in alignment, you will see that some of the things you yearned for had come into your life and you will also manifest things you didn't even know you wanted. So take a few minutes to think about your passions by starting with your interests. What do you enjoy doing in your spare time? If you had a day free of responsibilities, how would it unfold? And if you are lukewarm about everything, then do spend some time digging through your past, especially your childhood.

Now, after you have pondered your favorite things, take your notebook and write down ten things you want in your life right now. Examples of what you might find are that you want more time to relax, to eat more nutritiously, to be active and healthy, and to engage in outdoor activity. Many people are passionate about living a healthy lifestyle. Indeed, often we find we want simple things, but a more specific passion may seep out such as that you want to take art classes or practice yoga or make a career move or have another child. If you check your list periodically, you will find that new ideas arise, and you will begin to discover the passions that were hiding or that you had forgotten years ago. Writing a list is the first step. But to make things happen, you need to set intentions.

When you make your list, don't hold back. That is, if you think things might take too much time or that you don't have the skills or your desire seems, well, totally impossible, write it down anyway. The list will always be a work in progress, not a commitment. As you begin to work on your list, you may be thinking of the negative aspects of the goal and want to scratch it. Don't be so quick to do that. You may think the adventure could shake things up in your life in a bad way, but you don't know that. Everything we do is part of a larger scheme. We are inextricably linked and events have multiple ramifications. And anyway, the difficulties may be temporary so go with the flow. Follow your heart. Your intuition will guide you. Feel the freedom to write down what you want, blinders on. That is when the magic happens.

And it is important to keep in mind that manifesting is not a matter of wanting something and after a few steps, seeing it come into your life. Sure, you will get most of the things you go for, but when people are involved, they have their own desires, and maybe those desires do not mesh with yours. So if you finally tell your friend that you have feelings for her, and she does not feel the same way, it does not mean you will not find someone even better or that things will not change in the future. Go with the flow. Love fearlessly. You will get to a good place and things will happen, and when there are obstacles, you will grow from them. It's all a part of the process. Events will probably not occur exactly as you imagine, but if you live with courage and go for what you want, you will ultimately experience fulfillment and much greater joy in your life. Remember, there are other forces at work. Look for the synchronicities.

Flow Manifesting Step #2: Set intentions

Set an intention for two of the things on your list. Whatever your desires, make a list of all the things you need to do to make these a reality. Suppose you want a new career. Figure out everything needed from the first steps of obtaining education and certifications to steps needed to obtain employment. Research salaries and how such a job would fit into your lifestyle. And begin to take the necessary steps. The point is, if there is something that excites you, pursue it, even if it doesn't fit with your present experience and even if it does not seem possible. Do not shoot your dream down because you can think of many reasons why it wouldn't work. That's your ego. Just explore what you desire. Of course, your desires may change as you experience personal growth so be open to whatever comes up. Pursue these two goals fervently and don't give up unless you change your mind, which is perfectly fine and not uncommon. Desires change all the time!

Visit this portion of your notebook daily to see if there is anything you can do to move toward the goals. It is a good idea to set aside 30 minutes each day to work on steps associated with the goals, whether the steps include doing research, connecting with a particular individual or refining your strategy. Once you complete one of the goals on your list, cross it off and replace it with another one, so you will always have two things you can focus on. In addition to setting intentions, we suggest the use of affirmations--positive statements that reinforce the existence of a certain state of wellbeing-- specific to your goals. They will not only help to change your perspective and inject a bit of positivity into your life, they will also help you get what you want.

Flow Manifesting Step #3: Use affirmations the right way

Once you uncover some of your soul desires, and begin to take action to embrace them, you may need a little help getting them to materialize, especially if you have not eliminated most of the negative banter in your head. By now, if you have engaged in all of the practices so far, you are beginning to think more positively. You are letting life unfold, seeing people for who they are inside, while also realizing that you are communicating "ego to ego" quite often. But you are becoming more compassionate. You are forgiving human faults and getting along with people. You are probably less critical, more loving and more trusting as you begin to see that the universe is taking care of you. But you still notice that sometimes, you are angry or experience other negative emotions. We are human and the battle against negativity will always exist. So notice all the negative thoughts that go through your mind on a daily basis and write them down as you notice them. You may want to make a list on your phone so you can record them as they occur and later, transfer them to your notebook. After you write each negative thought, immediately write its direct opposite. These will become your affirmations. Affirmations are statements, asserting that the utterances are absolutely true.

Tweak your affirmations to ensure that they resonate with you, and that they are written in the present tense. That is, for such statements to impact your life, you have to presume that what you want is already happening. You need to feel that you are experiencing the manifestation of the desire right now. It may seem odd to say something is happening when that is not the case, but if you keep saying it in this manner, you will have a better chance of making it happen. We want you to love the words and really imagine how things will play out. If an affirmation does not feel right, don't use it. Change it to something that does.

Use the affirmations daily when you wake up in the morning, throughout the day whenever you think to do it, and before you go to bed. In this way, you are reprogramming your mind to believe that you have what you want, and the universe will respond to the feeling. An example of creating affirmations from your negative thoughts is that if your list looks like this:

I will never be able to afford a house.

I cannot find another job.

I don't have enough time for myself because I have too many responsibilities.

I'll never be able to master chess.

My health will only get worse.

Change it to this:

I have a new home that I love.
I have a job that I enjoy.
I have plenty of time for both my responsibilities and self-care.
I am an excellent chess player.
My body feels well.

Think about it. The first list includes tasks that seem insurmountable. It looks like you cannot afford a home and it is hard for you to get a job, and you just don't have time for anything. And to top it off, you suck at chess and you feel sick all the time. But the second list, which include your new affirmations, suggests that you are already living the dream.

Every day, people get new jobs and buy houses. And making time for yourself may mean doing self-care before you do the daily chores. Mastering a game or anything for that matter just takes a bit of practice. Illness often responds to positivity. Your initial list is riddled with fear and doubt but the second list conjures images of what you want, and includes things that will bring you joy. It is probably not what you are used to because you deliberately keep your expectations low. You don't want to be disappointed. But you need not worry about disappointment because disappointment manifests as multiple thoughts and feelings, which you are now able to keep in check with the processes we shared in Chapter Three. So be fearless and think those awesome thoughts, and let go of doubt. You really have nothing to lose. And you will turn your life around by flooding your brain with positivity.

Flow Manifesting Step #4: Make a mental movie

We encourage you to use your imagination. Imagination is the brain of the soul. It is the lifeblood of creative experience. It is the cosmic key that allows you to create the life you want. When you use your mind, you can imagine anything. There are no limits or restrictions. You can be anyone, have anything and play the part with perfection. What better way to use your imagination than to make a movie in your mind with you in the starring role? In fact, sport professionals know this trick well. Before a big game, they visualize how things will play out, and guess what? The game often does go exactly that way because the imagination is the most powerful tool you have to get what you want.

Even if you are not a sports superstar, you can make a mental movie. Imagine yourself going through your day, performing routine tasks, and seeing everything move flawlessly. While things are going so well in your mini-movie about your ordinary life, why not include some of the goals you've already set? In Flow Manifesting Step #2, we encouraged you to break your intentions down into manageable steps. Think about those steps. For example, you decided to go for the promotion so you imagine yourself walking into your boss' office and telling him why you deserve it. You are both smiling. You fast forward the movie to telling your friends the good news and even to the day that the promotion is announced. Because this is a goal, or something you want to manifest, thinking about the possibility will make you smile. If it does not make you happy, change your goal, but don't confuse worrying with a lack of desire. If you want something, it should feel good, but if worried thoughts intrude such as *how will my boss react, am I ready for the responsibility, do I have the skills for the new position*, realize that you are off track. And if you do find yourself worrying while living in your movie, go back to Chapter Three. Remember, you are human and are prone to go negative. But the more you tackle your negative thoughts and emotions, the quicker you will be able to make things happen through manifesting with the flow.

To use the mental movie technique, spend ten minutes in the morning--soon after you awake--imagining what you actually want to happen. It is a mini awake dream where you see yourself in the new model you created. What is happening? Who are you with? How do you feel? The movie can be about anything. You are the producer. You get to decide what to watch and how things will play out. Imagine the scenes each morning before you get out of bed, and then be cognizant of the signs in your life showing up as your intention starts to become a reality. It will likely not happen overnight, but your vision will begin to materialize as you move closer to it day by day.

Flow Manifesting Step #5: Live in the present

We talked about mindfulness in Chapter Four, and it is one of the most important things you can do to manifest the things you want and is an essential part of Flow Manifesting. In fact, if you take nothing else away from this book other than that, you will improve your life immensely, because the more you live in your head, the more likely it is that you will get tripped up. Again, we tend to think negatively, so no matter where you are on your spiritual journey, it is easy to fall into this trap. You may have done all of the exercises and use positive affirmations, but then you have this whole mind thing going on while you are in the shower, while you are watching television, while you are working and it is distracting. And this can happen even after you have been practicing intentional mindfulness and meditation for many years. So if you hold negative beliefs, they will plague you at any moment the ego is able to break through, and the secret to staying present is to recognize these disruptive thought forms as nothing more than the ego attempting to take over.

To reduce these disruptions, just consciously live in the moment and recognize the ego for what it is. Once you start to notice the ego and label it as "just my ego fighting for its life" or just my Monkey Mind, you will at least for a few minutes experience presence. This catching of the ego will occur over and over again, but the more you do it, the quicker you will recognize it so the stretches of mindfulness last longer. As time goes on you will be present much more frequently and the ego will be less problematic. It is a process and it does take practice, but the goal is to live in the present moment as much as possible.

You may have noticed through meditation and mindful living that you are starting to do this automatically. If so, bravo! Conscious awareness is critical to living your best life. When you are unconscious, you will act according to habit. For example, when you are in the present you will eat when you are hungry and stop before you are full, but if you are in your head, you are more likely to eat at rigid mealtimes and eat more than you really want. When you are present, you will get along better with others, but when you are not, you are more likely to think critically of other people. You get the picture. Being present in your life changes everything.

This step--to be present as much as possible-- is so important but perhaps the most difficult to achieve. The reason why it is critical is that if you listen to the banter in your head --the thoughts sound so logical, so right, they must be true--you might act on them and go down the wrong path. Of course, you need to discern when your ego is warning you of a real danger or if it is doing mental gymnastics in your head by leveraging the Monkey Mind. When you are rehashing things in your head, not sure what to believe, feeling angry or otherwise distraught, that is the ego wanting to be noticed. But when you are thinking with presence, the outcome of the thought feels right. Here, you are combining the intuition to come from the soul with your thoughtful conclusions. When you live in the present moment, you will do this more often. You can ignore the anger, or the story you make up about what is going on, and resolve situations logically and feel good about your choices.

While staying present through meditation or mindfulness is of the utmost importance to achieving awareness, the exercises we provide are important too. The ego needs to be dealt with on its own terms so while being present is necessary for getting in touch with the soul, it is also necessary to evaluate your life, change your thoughts, feel your feelings and have a better understanding of you as a full-fledged human being with a body and an ego in addition to a soul. Finally, the last Flow Manifesting step is about how to get more connected to the soul so you can more easily use your intuition.

Flow Manifesting Step #6: Ask for answers

For this step, we would like to add a little something to your meditation practice. We mentioned this in Chapter Four, but want to reiterate that prior to meditation, think of a question or concern. What do you really want to know right now? Then, let it go. You will receive an answer one way or another if you are open to it.

We want you to understand that answers do not always come as expected and in fact, will come in many forms. You may get an idea like a bolt of lightning. Suddenly, you just know. Or you may notice coincidences. Perhaps you are thinking of pursuing art, and then the next day you meet someone named Art, and then you pass an art store you did not know existed, and then when you turn on the television a show on artists just happens to be the first thing you see. That is the universe giving you a thumbs up. This does not necessarily mean you will ultimately become a great artist. Later, you may put your paintbrush down, but it is the road you are meant to take now. And there are other ways that answers may come such as being offered a new job that seemingly came out of the blue. You take it because you need the money, but it is something that perhaps answered a question you previously asked or fulfills a desire you have. Now, you are Flow Manifesting!

Everything you do is Flow Manifesting

Developing awareness or presence or whatever you want to call it is exhilarating. It frees you from the chains of your thinking mind. You know who you are, and you know that the conditioning your thinking mind has experienced is not you. You are not your thoughts, your opinions or your beliefs. You are a soul that is part of a larger picture. You are not alone, and while you are part of the collective, you have a unique essence. If you are discovering this for the first time, it is exciting, and you may want to use your notebook to record your dreams and goals or for journaling or for writing down synchronicities or intuitive hits. This way, you won't forget all the magic that is happening every day. You may also still want to write out your negative thoughts and emotions and keep making changes. Read your notebook every so often. You will begin to see the improvements in your life take shape.

While meditation and mindfulness is so so important to getting in touch with your higher self, there are other ways to access answers from spirit. You may want to use a Tarot deck or connect with your spirit guides or angels. Traditional psychotherapy may provide "aha" moments. Getting answers--knowing which life path to take or even which shoes to buy or which movie to watch--is very important to your soul growth. Everything that comes into your experience is not an accident.

Did you notice that we lumped in shoe shopping and film viewing with choosing a life path? And that is because everything you do is important. On a whim, you choose three-inch heels, even though you always wore flats. Sure, it makes you look good, but your feet hurt at the end of the day and you wonder if you should have been more thoughtful when you chose your footwear. You get the picture. Every decision you make has consequences. Had you been living your life in the present, you would have made the purchase with greater awareness, and the result would have been totally different. It is the same with choosing a movie. You might ask, how would that matter? After all, the movie is only a couple of hours long. True, but ideas become embedded in your consciousness. If you choose a comedy or a very depressing drama, and then you repeat a few times a month, think of what that does to your mindset. The comedies might lighten the mood, but the dark films will likely provoke negative thoughts. So make all of your decisions mindfully.

This is not to say that you should worry about every decision you make or never watch a negative television show for fear of what it will do to you. Fear and worry defeat the purpose and is always negative. We just want you to be centered and connected and joyful, and to choose what is best for you. And so, as you go about your life, consider your choices. Yes, use your mind to make decisions, but go beyond critical thinking and get in touch with your spiritual side.

For big decisions, you may want to spend a little more time researching and considering all of your options, or not. If you know the answer, dwelling on a choice can be counterproductive. Use your intuitive guidance always and move forward when you feel the time is right, while shutting out the well-meaning opinions of others. Remember this is your life. And sometimes, your decision may be not to make a decision at all. Sometimes, you may want to pause your decision, and at other times, you will want to just allow things to unfold.

For less complicated decisions, like choosing a chocolate or vanilla ice cream cone, you are just thinking hmmm, what am I really in the mood for? Then pause for a few seconds and see what you intuit. Sure, the choice seems trivial unless you are allergic to chocolate, but even for the little things, it does not hurt to hit pause. It is not satisfying to order something in a restaurant and by the time the food is served, you realize you are not in the mood for what you requested. Flow manifesting works best when you know what you really want through conscious awareness. And this sort of lifestyle comes with living mindfully as much as possible.

You are one with the universe

Dorothy, the protagonist in the *Wizard of Oz*, realized she had the power to go home all along, and that "aha" moment ended her quest. But that moment also began a new journey of self-discovery. She was just beginning to trust herself and this allowed the release of the fear she carried with her from Kansas. Had she known she had the power to change her life and that she did not need the help of the Wizard, her experience would have been vastly different. But as Glinda the Good Witch pointed out, while Dorothy could have gone home any time she wanted, she had to learn that for herself. Dorothy's journey is your journey. It is about going within, knowing who you are and finding your power. While reading this book will not change your life, asking the right questions and learning along the way through self-discovery will.

If there is one message we really want you to take away is that life can be easy. Live it with curiosity and don't take it too seriously. Your experience just is and it is better to move with the current than to fight against it. This mindset will emerge as you continue to practice presence, but it is a process. Be patient. Being energetically aligned in this way will help to make things happen and is the cornerstone of Flow Manifesting. Of course, we are only telling you what you already know. You have the joy and knowledge inside of you right now. You have the potential to do anything with this life that you want. And you had it all along, Dorothy. Everything you always wanted and needed is inside of you.

Sandrine Baptiste has relied on her inner knowing since she was a small child, something that defines her calling, which is to help people discover the gifts of looking within. Sandrine is a founder and managing partner at ENoetic Press where her connection to source drives every blog, publication and event, and where she is able to leverage her talent for verbal and written communication. She is also a holistic coach, where her passion for connecting with people culminates in extraordinary and lasting results. Originally from Toulouse, France, Sandrine currently resides in central New Jersey. She moved to the United States soon after completing her studies at the *Universite de Toulouse-le-Mirail,* where she majored in psychology.

Rhonda Tremaine has had a passion for astrology since she was a teenager. With assistance from the birth chart, she coaches individuals to explore their soul's evolution. Rhonda is also a founder and managing partner at ENoetic Press where she draws on her innate writing ability and love of marketing to help grow the business. Her commitment to helping others through promoting self-knowledge comes through in her work on the Everything Noetic blog, her books, and her astrological perspective. Rhonda has always lived in the New York City metropolitan area. She studied sociology at the City University of New York's Brooklyn College.

CPSIA information can be obtained
at www.ICGtesting.com
Printed in the USA
LVHW081355070422
715596LV00008B/419